CW01067093

FROM
WILDERNESS
TO
WONDER

Why I fell in love with God.

Wilma J. Lansdell

WESTBOW°
PRESS
A DIVISION OF THOMAS NELSON
& ZONDERVAN

Scriptures taken from the Holy Bible, New International Version®, NIV®.
Copyright © 1973, 1978, 1984, 2011 by Biblica, Inc.™ Used by permission of
Zondervan. All rights reserved worldwide. www.zondervan.com The "NIV"
and "New International Version" are trademarks registered in the United
States Patent and Trademark Office by Biblica, Inc.™ All rights reserved.

Scripture quotations taken from the New American Standard Bible®,
Copyright © 1960, 1962, 1963, 1968, 1971, 1972, 1973, 1975, 1977, 1995 by
The Lockman Foundation. Used by permission." (www.Lockman.org)

Scripture taken from the King James Version of the Bible.

WestBow Press books may be ordered through booksellers or by contacting:

WestBow Press
A Division of Thomas Nelson & Zondervan
1663 Liberty Drive
Bloomington, IN 47403
www.westbowpress.com
1 (866) 928-1240

Because of the dynamic nature of the Internet, any web addresses or
links contained in this book may have changed since publication and
may no longer be valid. The views expressed in this work are solely those
of the author and do not necessarily reflect the views of the publisher,
and the publisher hereby disclaims any responsibility for them.

Any people depicted in stock imagery provided by Thinkstock are models,
and such images are being used for illustrative purposes only.
Certain stock imagery © Thinkstock.

ISBN: 978-1-4908-4820-4 (sc)
ISBN: 978-1-4908-4821-1 (hc)
ISBN: 978-1-4908-4819-8 (e)

Library of Congress Control Number: 2014914802

Printed in the United States of America.

WestBow Press rev. date: 9/24/2014

Contents

DEDICATION

This book is dedicated to my seven great-grandchildren, Bayleigh and Madison and Shiloh and Peyton and Damon and Ella and Maya Faith. It is also dedicated to those of mine as yet unborn. If you are my great-grandchild and your name is not above, then I give you permission to take a pencil or a crayon or a marker and write it on the line that I have left just for you, _____. I will be watching for your name.

FOREWORD

If you were to meet Wilma Lansdell on the street or in the grocery store today, you would mistakenly think she was a quiet, shy, retiring "older" woman. How wrong your perceptions would have been!! While looking rather conservative and "stiff-upper-lippish" on the outside, she is actually one of the most passionate fireballs I have ever met! With a tender heart and a hand that is most at home when holding someone else's, Wilma showers love and attention on others without demanding she be the centre of attention.

The "engine" for her caring spirit is her close relationship with Jesus Christ. I have personally and repeatedly witnessed the genuineness of Wilma's faith; it is a living, breathing, intimate communion with her Saviour that has no room for squabbles about doctrine or denominations. In fact, she told me recently that the perfect name for a church would be "The Gathering Of People Who Love God And Each Other." To Wilma (and to myself as well), that is all that really matters! See what Jesus says in Matthew 22:37-40!

My family has been blessed on countless occasions by Wilma's wonderful down-home cooking! She and her dear husband Clyde have a special ministry of hospitality, blessing others by opening up their home on a regular basis. Even though hampered by poor eyesight, Wilma continues to excel not only in the kitchen but also in the nursing home room, around the small group circle and even on the quilting rack.

You may or may not agree with everything Wilma says in this book but one thing I know for sure: everything she has written here comes from a heart that grapples with, meditates on, prays about and honestly contemplates the transcendent realities of God, His Word and the sometimes rocky roads that believers in Jesus Christ are called to walk on our way Home! I trust this book helps you to not only fall deeper in love with God but with this wonderful woman as well!

Bruce Jones, Pastor of Meaford Olivet Baptist Church

Meaford, ON, Canada

ACKNOWLEDGEMENTS

My deepest thanks goes to my God who showed up so regularly in the early hours of the morning, who allowed me in these visits to get to know Him in ways I never had before, who often came into my awareness in strange places like motion lights on a garage door, in the daily doings of an orchid or on a train half way across my country. I'm glad You cared enough about me, dear God, to make Yourself available in all these ways.

Thank you to Clyde, my husband of almost 58 years, who has made the journey with me, who never gave up on me, never gave up on himself, but more importantly, never gave up on God.

Thank you to my sons, Roger and Rayburn, who are their own persons working out their own faith, and this makes me proud. I thank them as well for presenting me with the two daughters I never had, Sandy and Sharon, without question the most wonderful daughters-in-law in the world.

Thank you to my grandchildren, six in all, who are all doing good things with their lives--thanks to Kyle and Jessica, to Devon and Nathan, to Bryce and Alysha. And thank you to four in-law grandchildren that I dearly love--Anna and Carl, Briar and Katlyn.

Thank you to Bruce Jones for the Foreword for this book. He has been a true pastor whose care for us, frequently, has been what has kept us going. We count him and his family among our dearest friends.

Thank you to Phyllis Stanley who told me at the beginning of this project to write with publishing in mind. She walked with me all the way to the end. Thank you to Dorothy Dennis, who read as I wrote and was the biggest cheerleader a body could ever have. Thank you to Donna Jansen and Patricia Ellis who also read as I wrote and gave me the feedback I needed to hear. And thank you to Nita Irwin whose computer savvy surpasses mine, and she was willing to help me just when I needed it.

Thank you to Oswald Chambers, long gone from this earth but who said while he was here, "The questions that truly matter in this life are remarkably few, and they are all answered by these words--'Come to Me.'" It is this statement and others like it that have sent me back to the pages of his devotional book My Utmost For His Highest almost every morning for the last fourteen years. They are always new every morning.

Thank you to Amazon for making my Kindle available to me. Without it there likely would not have been a book.

Thank you Maurice Broaddus, Jenn Seiler and Mary Wegener and the good folks at Westbow Press, who took my child, cleaned the smudges off her face and hands, dressed her up in a lovely new dress and sent her out to face the world on her own. Bless your journey, little one, and may you be a blessing to someone you meet along your way.

INTRODUCTION

It is early morning, October 10, 2013. How does one know when one begins any project whether the motives are pure, the goal honourable? I don't know. I only know that for a long time I felt compelled to put pen to paper, to record my thoughts. I only know that many have said, "You should write a book". I read a phrase just yesterday that hit a chord in my heart--"You are at the crossroads of your here and now." (Kapat-Zinn, 2010) So here I sit in this early morning quiet, in the early throes of my 78th year, so thankful to my Father for where I am that I must write it down. He has truly slogged it out with me through the wilderness of self and shown me a glimmer of His wonder. What might come of this project, I can't imagine. But if you ever see it, please know that it was God who led me to this place.

CHAPTER 1

I am who I am

MEDITATION: To thine own self be true and it must follow as the night the day, thou cans't not then be false to any man.... (Shakespeare, 2003)

My name is Wilma. I would rather it had been Shelaine. I was born in the house my Grandfather built on Manitoulin Island, but it might have been better if I had been born somewhere else. You see, I was exposed to two people, right after my birth, whose "not feeling well"-ness was soon diagnosed as polio. One passed away; one lived to later marry my aunt, but he forever bore the scars of the disease. My mother was always sure that I had been affected by the contact. I don't know. I only know that for all of my life my legs have hurt. My clothes were never quite as nice as the other kids in school; I never seemed to have as much fun as the other kids; and on and on.... You get the gist.

Florence Littauer in her book <u>Personality Plus for Couples</u> (Littauer 2001) classifies my personality type as Melancholy Perfectionist. The details of every situation are important to me, and I would like them to be, if not perfect, at least nice. As a result, melancholia has been my constant companion. Dissatisfaction, discouragement and disappointment have dogged my path every step of the way. How could they not have? Dissatisfaction because life is never perfect; discouragement because I am never perfect; disappointment because others are never perfect.

The vagaries of life

We spent the evening last night with dear friends living with the recent diagnosis of cancer. That this diagnosis is already having a physical, emotional and spiritual impact on their lives was evident. I was humbled by their courage and honesty. After their departure I then watched some news which seemed to be filled with the sexual promiscuity of those in high places and the slippery slope that choice had sent them down. Then came the greed--the greed of those in high places and many others besides, a greed that is slowly but surely driving whole countries into chaos. Thus it was a muddled mind that I put to pillow last night, inviting sleep; but it wasn't long until the "since time began God" principle drifted through my consciousness--"Every Knee Will Bow." It is not a matter of IF, only of WHEN. My prayer is that the WHEN will come for myself, for my grandchildren, and for every other human on this planet early enough in the journey along the path to our own death, that we will have time to experience the unspeakable peace and joy that God wants us to experience. (Written in 2011)

How does God work in a life to bring one to her knees? There is a theory out there that the world, as we know it, began with a BIG BANG. I care not to discuss the hows or whys of creation. I wasn't there nor do I know anyone who was. The omniscient, omnipotent, omnipresent God has all the details and will put an end to the argument in His own good time. I do know, however, that God sent me down a spiritual path that I had never been on with a BIG BANG. Oh, there were little forays into finding the God I wanted to know in my yearning heart. I remember going down the aisle, tears streaming down my cheeks, feeling so strongly in my young heart that there was something out there that I was missing from my life. This was a common practice in the fellowship I was a part of in the early Fifties. I tried to convey my feelings to the attending minister and was publicly congratulated for being such a good "church" kid. So life went on--and I remained a good "church" kid.

In due course the good, little "church" kid married-- married a preacher. And like most other young girls of that era, she believed that this step would lead directly to joy and peace.

"I will instruct you and teach you in the way you should go. I will counsel you with my loving eye on you." Psalm 32:8 (NIV)

It would be a long time before I would see the circumstances that I found myself in as God's way of teaching me what He wanted me to know. It would be a long time before I saw God at all.

So, life went on. I birthed two boys, loved them in my way, felt a huge responsibility to make them into the kind of people I felt they should be. I felt the same responsibility to the churches we served, and so I did the only thing I knew to do. I played my part in the programs that were designed to make a church grow. I gathered people around my table in the hope they would become part of the program. Oh, I liked these people. Many of them have become my best friends over the years. But, God! Where was God in it all? Thus, the ensuing years brought more church work, growing of boys, university degrees for husband, marrying of boys, entering of grandchildren, and in time, earning of money--way more than I had ever been used to. Life seemed good.

I was at the stage in my life where I had enough money, had enough freedom from family responsibility (nobody home but me and husband) to do some things I loved to do. I remember taking a friend and her little girl to a children's play at a nice, big theatre in a neighboring city on a very rainy Sunday afternoon. It was just one of those days for Nathasha. The words most frequently emanating from her mother's mouth were "Natasha, do" or "Natasha, don't." In due time, I said to Natasha, "Natasha, what will you call your little girl some day?" Her answer: "Laura." And so I said, "Natasha, you will only turn around three more times until you will be saying, "Laura, do" or "Laura, don't." It wasn't many days until Natasha said to me: "Aunt Wilma, I turned all the way around three times and I didn't growed a bit."

I have shared this funny little experience with many over the years. I love a story!! Natasha is a grown woman with her own family now living far away--a family I don't know, but the little girl she was is still a memory close to my heart. Does she know the joy she brought to a lady in her life all those years ago and the memory of which still does? I don't know. The greater question is do we see God at work in these ordinariest of experiences that come our way. I didn't--and continued to "didn't" for a long time. Still don't, as I want to. Seeing God in every step, in every circumstance, at all times, is hard work.

"...faith brings us into the right relationship with God and gives Him His opportunity to work. Yet God frequently has to knock the bottom out of your experience to get you into direct contact with Himself." (Chambers, 1963) It was in 1993 that I had my "bottom out of your experience" experience. I remember so many feelings from that time. I remember feeling like I was in a deep, dark pit trying desperately to claw my way to the top, but every time I would get my fingers just over the edge of the pit, some new development would send me to the bottom again. I remember saying to myself over and over, "What did I ever do to deserve this?" I remember thinking one day, "Hey, I bet I know what is going on. There is a giant battle going on out there in the cosmos between God and Satan and I am part of the battle;" but that didn't work well for me. It only made me mad at God. After a while more of Oswald Chambers' words pierced my heart: "If God can accomplish His purpose in this world through a broken heart, then why not thank Him for breaking yours."

(Chambers 1963) I am so thankful that somewhere along the way my cry became "Lord, what do You want me to learn from this?" And He has taught me. Oh! How He has taught me--and is still teaching me!

It was only just recently that a young man who was going through his own hell of anguish and pain, a young man searching for the "why", who asked, "What did you do?'" What did I do? No one had ever asked me that before-- not what did you do? Few ever asked me, "How did you feel", never mind "What did you do?" So I struggled to answer. Finally I said, "I got up every morning and went to work."

FB Post - May 26, 2013

"But Mary treasured up all these things and PONDERED them in her heart." Luke 2:19 (NIV) Pondered – I love that word. I love the look on the face of a pondering child. I love the words from the mouth of a pondering grown-up. Isn't it interesting that God chose a "pondering" heart in which to do such a mighty work? Is His Spirit searching the face of this earth right now for a pondering heart in which to do some mighty work? I suspect so. Could He do a mighty work in my pondering heart? I hope so. I need Him to.

My God pondering goes on.

Is that part of what God uses to see us through the heartbreaks of our lives--the ordinary? Is that how He brings peace and joy to a peace-and-joy-starved heart-- through the ordinary? Does He put us in a place, after putting us in THE PLACE where we cry with Peter, "To whom shall we go?" Does He give us the ability to see Him when we see two little girls sound asleep, crowded into the same crib just because they love each other, and our first thought is that God wants us to be that way with each other--to share in His deep love even though we are different? Does He give us the ability through our pain to look at someone else's pain with a quiet assurance that God's grace can take that hurtful experience and put her in a better place than she has ever been, not in spite of the pain, but because of the pain?

This is my story--my journey through pain toward the heart of God. I am 77 years old as I write this. I expect the "journey through" to last until the journey ends. Only then will I fully understand the absolute ugliness of the "wilderness" and know the absolute beauty of the "wonder."

CHAPTER 2

No song of my own

MEDITATION: Every sin is an attempt to fly from emptiness. (Weil, 2003)

FB Post: November 2, 2013

Husband and I had a discussion recently about addiction and how it works. He talked about our "besetting sin" or "the sin that so easily entangles" (Hebrews 12:1-2, NIV). These verses go on and admonish us to "fix our eyes on Jesus." I have heard faith described as the gaze of the soul upon God. Gaze--an interesting word not heard frequently in our day and time. Definition: "look steadily and intently, especially in admiration, surprise or thought." As these things rolled around in my head, I wondered if it could be so--that in the moments, in the circumstances that we cannot or do not see God, feel God, that those moments are the very beginning of our addiction, the moment that we begin to seek comfort in something other than God. And that slippery serpent knows. Oh! He knows so well that the seeking will only bring more pain. And the chaos will rule the day.

It was a Sunday. Life's circumstances had not been kind to me in recent months, so it was with eyes blurred by tears that I tried to put the finishing touches on Sunday dinner. That was when I noticed the red-winged blackbird perched on the high wire outside my kitchen window. The brilliance of the red and yellow of his wings in contrast to the ebony black of the rest of his body was stunning. Then, as quickly as he had appeared, he was gone, and for a second or two there was a blur of I knew not what in the area where he had been. Next, his spot on the high wire was occupied by none other than a mockingbird, and the beautiful blackbird was nowhere in sight. Why did the mockingbird choose that exact spot as his when the high wire stretched for several hundred feet?

I contemplated that scene for a long time. What makes the mockingbird so mean? I remembered watching one day as the mockingbird flew down on the patio outside my den window, only to chase away every bird feeding on the dropped seeds *so* that he could stand guard. He didn't pick up a seed and enjoy it himself, only guarded what he perceived as his domain, so that none other could enjoy it. Again, I ask, what makes the mockingbird so mean? Could it be that he has no song of his own? My internet info tells me that the mockingbird is capable of mimicking the songs of at least two hundred birds, but his own song he never sings. He has amazing talent, indeed, but could it be the root of his meanness?

My mind has come back and back to this scene for several years, and I have wondered over and over again if there is a spiritual lesson to be found in what I witnessed. A recent sermon that I was privileged to hear began with the question: Why do you go to church? It is a good question, one that we all should wrestle with. Am I there because it is what I have always done but have never really searched deep in the recesses of my own heart to decide what my faith is? Am I there because there I find the people that I have always known and I am comfortable with them? Robert Capon has described the church as a community of astonished hearts." One of the dictionary meanings of astonished is "struck dumb with wonder." Wow!! Have I ever felt struck dumb with wonder for what God has done for me? And If I have felt that and then came to share it with those of like mind, can you imagine what a gathering that would be? Would there be room for mediocrity, any bickering or bitterness, resentment or ridicule? Or would all gathered be so filled with praise that all who observed would KNOW that there was a sweet, sweet spirit in this place? We sing the old song, "This is my story, this is my song, praising my Saviour all the day long." That would encompass all of every day. It would leave little time for the negative things that often fill my life. More and more I am feeling that unless I develop a deep personal relationship with God, the song that I sing will be like the mockingbird's, not my own, and will likely do for me what the mockingbird's seemingly does for him--make me mean.

How do we catch a glimpse of who God really is? In his introduction to the book of Isaiah in The Message, Eugene Peterson has this to say: "The God of whom the prophets speak is far too large to fit into our lives. If we want anything to do with God, we have to fit into Him. They (the prophets) plunge us into mystery, immense and staggering." (Peterson, 2006) It is the awesomeness of this God that should drive us to our knees in fear but at the same time bring us an immeasurable peace, for in the midst of our Godly fear we know this God well enough to know that at the end of each day He is there to cradle us in his arms, to cry with us at the injustices of the day, to laugh with us at the joys we experienced and to kiss us softly "goodnight" as one who loves us.

Psalm 33:1 says, "Good people, cheer God! Right-living people sound best when praising." In Psalm 34:2, David says, "I live and breathe God." (Peterson, 2006) I have decided (and I realize that I may be wrong) that it would be impossible for me to develop a life of true praise without looking deep within myself to ascertain the areas of my life where Satan is in control, and as I have continued to contemplate this thought, it brings another question. I wonder what I would be like if Satan had no influence in my life. Since I am made in the image of God (Genesis 1:27), if I became more aware of the ways that Satan wins in my life, with the help of God's grace and the Holy Spirit, I should become more and more who He created me to be.

Come with me again, if you will, to my Alabama home, not to the high wire this time, but to the tree line along the edge of the property. The little towhee made his home in that tree line, going about the business of his life. I watched one day as he worked, his little feet flying as fast as the best kilted Scotsman's doing the highland fling would have. He worked diligently to unearth any errant bug or scattered seed hidden under the mat of dead leaves and debris that lined the fence. He seemed totally unaware that two fat mourning doves were enjoying the fruits of his labor behind him; he paid no attention to the nervy brown thrush who landed right beside him and quickly gobbled down anything that came his way; nor did the bevy of tufted titmouse who flew in and out enjoying the seeds bother him. He just went on being who God had created him to be.

That is what I want for myself--to be aware that God made me for a purpose, to bring glory to His name, to defeat as much as possible the influence of Satan in my life, and to go about doing those things that He meant for me to do without seeking recognition for any of it.

I don't know when my fingers touched the keys to type the above. I know it has rattled around in the bowels of at least two computers, and I know when I saw it. It was 1994. I had asked God again and again, "What do you want me to learn from this?" I had never dreamed He would use a mockingbird and a towhee to teach me so much.

A long time ago I received information that came seven miles across Lake Nipissing to my North Bay home that I should pick up a man at the dock and take him to the hospital. How I got that message in the days before cell phones, I can't remember. I did pick him up and took him to the hospital. He needed to go there because he had a fishhook in his nose with inches of fish line hanging down over his mouth and chin. As we waited, a nurse walked up and said, "What can I do for you?" The answer from the man was, "Oh, nothing. I like the fishhook in my nose." We have laughed often over this story and told it often. I love a story.

In Mark 10 (NIV), we see into the life and heart of a man named Bartimaeus, a blind man who sat begging by the roadside. Jesus and his disciples were leaving the city, followed by a large crowd, along the road where Bartimaeus was sitting. Verse 47 reads, "When he heard it was Jesus of Nazareth". Amazing! How did he hear that from his spot on the side of the road? How could he possibly hear over the din of the disciples and the large crowd leaving the city? Did the great God of the universe see deep into his heart and know it and give him the gift of heightened awareness in yet another sense? I don't know, but he heard. And he knew he needed mercy and he wasn't too proud to ask. But then came a Jesus question...a nurse kind of question. Jesus said, "What do you want?" Wouldn't it have been pretty obvious what he would want? I wonder for how many days after did those looking on tell the story and perhaps laugh a bit at the ludicrousness of it; but is it the question I must answer if I really want out of the pit?

I know what it is like not to see very well. I am the lady who steps up to (or so she thinks) her gray-headed husband and says, "I am ready to go when you are," and the answer comes back, "Well, you won't be going with me." It came from the mouth of a bald-headed man. See! How badly do

I want to see? How badly do I want that deep relationship with God? Is my melancholy perfectionist nature expecting a perfect relationship void of discouragement, dissatisfaction or disappointment--the three big D's in my life? It's THE question I must answer.

Only lately has Matthew 11:29-30 begun to haunt the dark shadows of the night and occupy my mind until morning light: "Take my yoke upon you and learn from me, for I am gentle and humble in heart, and you will find rest for your souls. For my yoke is easy and my burden is light." (NIV) The whole verse is a conundrum. If Jesus really wanted us alongside Him, would He not have made the invitation more palpable? And how do you find rest in a yoke? How do you get comfortable so you can rest carrying a burden? If you make a yoke easy, is it still a yoke and if you lighten a burden, can you still call it a burden? Hmmm....

"There are songs that can only be learned in the valley. No art can teach them; no rules of voice can make them perfectly sung. Their music is in the heart. They are songs of memory, of personal experience. They bring out their burden from the shadow of the past; they mount on the wings of yesterday." (Cowman, 2004)

The path from the wilderness to wonder is hard! It has many setbacks, takes much time. It took the Israelites 40 years. But if I want out of the pit (and I do--it is much too black in the pit), I must stay on the path. I will take one more step.

CHAPTER 3

My ugly orchid

MEDITATION: A bruised reed he will not break, and a smoldering wick he will not snuff out. Isaiah 42:3 (NIV)

FB Post May 18.2013

"'Consider the lilies of the field, how they grow, they neither toil nor spin'...they simply are! Think of the sea, the air, the sun, the stars and moon ...all of these simply are as well... yet what a ministry and service they render on our behalf"... Oswald Chambers. (1963)

As I lifted my head to contemplate what I had read the sun was beginning to shimmer on the Red Maple leaves outside my window. Only a day or so ago, life, of colour, of HOPE for tomorrow. I was looking at the face of God--full of LOVE looking back at me.

In March of 2008, in response to a death in the family, a dear friend brought me an orchid. This little plant had three blooms on it; they stayed for a long, long time, then one by one fell off. Not knowing, for sure, what to expect, I carefully watered the little plant regularly and was greatly excited when a new shoot came forth from the stem. Even though it didn't look a lot like the stem that had produced the three flowers, I was sure that was what it must be so I carefully tied the little shoot so it would grow up, though its natural bent was to grow straight west from the stem. The little sprout headed upward with a westerly veer to its growth and, after I don't know how much time, the original stem produced two more blooms.

These little blooms did their part to brighten my life for several weeks and then one by one fell off. So what would come next? It was several weeks later that I noticed a fat, fleshy sprout heading west from the stem. Soon there were several headed in all four directions and places in between. What are these things? What are they for? I decided they must be roots that would eventually bury themselves in the soil and the plant would grow a lot bigger. But I did not want a bigger plant!! I had no place to put it.

At this point I called the Florist's Shop and spoke to someone in her employ. I asked if it would be okay just to cut them all off. "Oh, no!" she said, "You might kill the plant." Though she was certain that "cut off" these ugly shoots would be the demise of the plant, she was not sure what they were. She suggested I bring it in and let the florist tell me. So that was the plan!

In the meantime, however, a neighbor had given me a pretty outer pot for my little orchid. My decision was, since I couldn't cut them off, I didn't have to look at them. So I stuffed them all down between the two pots. Out of sight, out of mind! It was many weeks before I took my orchid to the florist.

When she saw what I had done she was aghast. "The plant can't breathe." she said as she pulled them all out. I brought my plant home with tentacles sticking out every which direction. Ugly, yes! But now they could feed the plant.

One day when I was "ugh"-ing how much I disliked the look of these shoots, I couldn't help but think what a great illustration of the hurt and pain in my life they represented. Hurt and pain are neither pretty nor comfortable, but there is no doubt in my mind that they are necessary. I know of no character in the Bible who fulfilled the great purposes of God outside of pain. When we think about it for just a minute, it doesn't take long to realize that the pain came from diverse sources: Joseph from the mistreatment of others but whose pain served to illustrate the providence of God; Job from intense physical and mental pain, which if not caused by God, certainly used by God to sear on the hearts of those who will listen the absolute sovereignty of God; David whose hurt and pain, for the most part, was the product of his own sinfulness. Yet, David's pain and sorrow have been, down through the ages, the stellar example of God's forgiveness second only to the Cross of Christ

As humans, very much as I did with the ugly orchid tentacles, we try to hide the hurt and pain of our lives-- the pain of our own failures, the pain of betrayal by others, the pain of loss of all sorts of things (job, finances, children gone from home, death of someone we love and so on), and the disappointment in just life itself. The result is much like the result when I tried to hide the ugly tentacles of my orchid. Our soul can't breathe!

Let's go back to 1994 or thereabouts. I am still pleading: "Lord, what do you want me to learn from all of this?" Still standing in the footprints of Bartimaeus, blind and fogged up, naked and cold, crying I want to see. The tentacles of fear, of rejection, of an uncertain future, of loss, of shame; all these I tried to keep shoved down between my two pots--the pot of who I really was right then and the pot of who I thought I needed to be if I was ever to get out of the pit.

Oh, there were cracks of light that made their way into the pit--lots of them. I remember a Sunday--a Sunday locked down in a snowstorm that had paralyzed our community, and in the midst of this my phone rang. It was an Alabama brother calling. When he heard my distress he immediately said, "We will come." Come! Even hearing about a Canadian winter usually sent them into an aura of amazement that any person in his right mind would even think of living a life in those circumstances. Commit to come in the middle of a snowstorm!! But come they did.

I remember the phone ringing on another Sunday. It was an older couple (older to us then, likely the age we are right now, which no longer seems old) inviting us for tea and a visit. A visit? What did they want to visit about? Did they want to peek into the details of our pain, to pass out advice, to rebuke or what? We went. The gentleman loved music, husband loves music. And so they sat on a piano bench, two humans made in the image of God, two human spirits marred by the troubles of this world, and they shared a common love, the love of music. In due course they served us tea. Tea that warmed our bodies and our hearts, fed us to add a little strength and sent us on our way. No advice, no rebuke, no glossing over the ugly--just the gift of themselves and their time. I love a story. I especially love this story. I often hear the phrase "I will pray for you" and that is good; but when I think of this couple, I am left to wonder: Can God use our prayers if they are not accompanied by the gift of ourselves?

FB Post - June 22, 2013

We all have a story. Some stories are seemingly pretty, at least to the onlooker, from beginning to end. Others not so much. But approached in the right way, each story can give us a better understanding of who God is, can give us a wee glimpse of His purpose in this world. And our story is given deeper meaning if someone else wants to hear it in order to help them in the writing of their own. Nothing is wasted in God's economy!

So, what to do with the "tentacles"--the tentacles of fear, of doubt, of what to do next? Should I tuck these feelings inside my two pots or put them out there, with the trust that God would use them to help me "breathe"?

Somewhere along on my journey I read again the story of David and Uzzah. Poor Uzzah! Killed for touching the Ark of the Covenant, killed for trying to help. In II Samuel 6: 1-11, the story of Uzzah is a familiar one in the teachings I heard at my pre-teen Bible camp. Was it told so often because the teachers liked the feeling of all those Zeds rolling off their tongue? Or was it because they felt it was important they guide me to live my life "right", keep all the commandments "right"? My *again* reading of this story would come many years later and would come from the depths of the "pit". Funny how, when the circumstances of a life drive us to our knees crying to God for help, we are no longer so certain about the things we always thought we knew. I began to wonder about David in this story. He was the king, had command of the men he gathered up to do what he wanted to see done. He knew God's instruction as to how the ark was to be carried. Yet he ignored it and provided a new cart for its transport. This "man after God's own heart" seemingly ignored what he knew God's instruction to be and did it his own way, but he wasn't killed like Uzzah. How come? How come???

These could have been dangerous musings for an emotionally malnourished mind like mine was just then. I am so thankful to God that He stepped in, took my mixed up thoughts and feelings and set me on the road to "wonder". That is exactly what happened. This was the beginning of my journey to "wonder", not the wondering, "I just have to know" mindset as to what is "right", and then when I decide what I think is right, my "God" goes in that box where I can manage Him. Rather it was a journey not to "knowing" but to "believing"--not to a intellectual belief but a feeling belief that God had a plan for me, that He cared about me, that He would work things out to draw me to Him and make me more like Jesus. It was and still is a weak, faltering journey. Satan gets the best of me again and again, but that is when I am reminded that there are lots of times when only God's grace will do. And I am thankful. Those ugly tentacles are out in the open and helping me breathe.

FB Post - Nov. 7, 2013

My little dog didn't have a very good day on Sunday. He didn't want to move and if we tried to move him he squealed loudly. That there was pain was obvious. Monday morning he went to the vet. Turns out he has a bad back. Prescription-- pain medicine and no running or jumping for two weeks. I guess, even though he still likes to run and play, he is getting old like everything else in this house. What is interesting to me is how quickly he has learned to come close to me and turn his little bum around to just the right position for me to pick him up in the way the vet said to. It dawned on me in the wee hours of this morning that maybe that is exactly what God wants from me. Nothing too attractive about a bum--nothing too attractive about our human "uglies". Does He want us to come to Him with the ugliest that is in us, present it to Him, and let Him pick us up and put us in a place of rest, peace and beauty? It was Paul who said, "For when I am weak, then I am strong." 2 Corinthians 12:10 (NIV)

CHAPTER 4

Three blind mice

Meditation: Watching a husband with cancer sing a love song to his wife makes you phone home to say "I love you." A little perspective is a good thing. – Terral McBay

Three blind mice, three blind mice,

See how they run, see how they run.

They all take after the farmer's wife,

She cut off their tails with a carving knife,

Did you ever see such a sight in your life,

As three blind mice.

Now why would I wake up this morning with this ditty playing around in the recesses of my mind, a ditty that was common to hear quoted by Daddy or Mom in my childhood, but one which I doubt I have thought of in over 60 years? As I pondered this, some interesting thoughts came into my mind.

I have no idea when the above words found their way to a page that has been buried in the bowels of my computer ever since. I dig them out now to share with you.

Before I do, however, I also need to share a disclaimer. Anything you read in the following is not a representation of how I feel about a "farmer's wife". Couldn't be! My mother was one. Perhaps the only reason I never made that high calling was because I wasn't smart enough.

I was likely in my early teens when I realized my younger sister, who would have been eight, could milk a cow just as efficiently and just as fast as my mother. This noble accomplishment was not one that I particularly aspired to, but to be left in the dust by one so much my junior was not good. So my Daddy assigned me a cow. I picked up a pail, I picked up a stool and proceeded to tackle the task at hand. It shouldn't be that hard! I had watched either my mother or my dad milk a cow for lo! these many years. So I sat down in the right position, grabbed one of those long, hanging appendages of flesh and yanked for all I was worth.

Success! A stream of white liquid rattled its way to the bottom of my pail. It was followed by another. Soon my pail had a respectable amount of milk in it and it was coming from the cow in an ever decreasing stream. I decided that was enough. I would quit and quit I did.

The next day I took up my station and went through the same process. It wasn't many days until my efforts proved futile; that cow would not give one drop of milk. Now why did she do that? Because, apparently, I had left a cup or so of milk in that big milk container each time. I had caused the cow to dry up. My Dad was not pleased. I was banished from that stool to never return again. That is why I say I wasn't smart enough to be a farmer's wife!

Back to those mice of the little ditty!

I wondered in that early morning hour, when it ran through my head, what its meaning could possibly be. Who wrote it and what was he or she thinking when writing it? Mr. Wikipedia tells me that the little rhyme was first published in England in 1609, and the possible author might be a Thomas Ravenscroft who was a teenager at the time. It didn't make its way into children's literature until 1842. I cannot know what the author might have been thinking, but here are some thoughts that wandered into my head in that early morning hour.

I wondered why the blind mice ever got close to the farmer's wife in the first place. Did the warmth of her farm kitchen stove lure them or was it the smell of what she might have been cooking on that stove? Or was she the one who saw them and lured them to her side with big hunks of cheese for the express purpose of doing them in? I doubt that any of these ramblings are too important in the grand scheme of things, but as my mind wandered I couldn't help but think how like those mice we humans are. Or, at least, this one...!

The Bible tells us that God's Spirit bears witness with our spirit that we are His children. This says to me that I should know instinctively when my thoughts, my words, my actions are not those produced by God's Spirit within me; but how often do I rush into danger to satisfy some physical urge, to bring comfort from my own lack of self-worth? Or how often is it simply Satan luring me with the "cheese" that he knows is my greatest temptation? We are all, then quite like the three mice--plagued with blindness, spiritual blindness, and thus we lose our "tails."

If I could interview that farmer's wife from the 17th century, I would ask her why she didn't cut their heads off and be done with it. I would also ask if she cut the whole tail off at once or waited to do a second lop as those poor, dumb mice made a second circle around the hem of her skirt. Poor, dumb mice! How like them we are. And all to seek our own comfort!

I read somewhere just a while ago that Jesus' temptations fell into three categories as do all of ours: 1) Performance, 2) Possessions, and 3) What others think of us. Oh, I had often heard the temptations of Jesus categorized in theological words, but never did they sear my heart, fly deep into the depths of my consciousness with no intent of being removed easily like these words did. Comfort! The things we go after for our own comfort. Does this mean "possessions" are wrong, or "performance"? Should I not want to do well? What about caring about what others think? Is that not the caring that produces kindness, gentleness, even love? Even our prayers, often, are a plea to God for something that we think will bring us comfort.

I know a little three year old girl who was taken from the tub after her bath by her Mommy, dried off and her naked bum set down on the bathroom counter for the hair brushing. She sat still for a moment but her sitting-still time was about gone when she said, "Mommy, if I don't soon get off this counter I am going to be stuck here forever. And then all I will ever be is a bathroom decoration." Is that what we are? Naked decorations in this world, seeking so earnestly our own comfort, stuck with the view of the world and ourselves that we have always had and blinded to the nature of God, the will of God, the goodness of God that comes in all kinds of unsuspecting ways at all kinds of unsuspecting times?

God wants us to SEE HIM!

FB post - Nov. 14, 2013

It was 4:20 AM when I pushed the "start" button on the coffee pot. I sat down in my chair to wait for it to percolate. It was black outside my window! It was quite black inside my heart! The reason for my "inside" blackness? My own mistakes! It took only a minute for me to realize that the two lights on each side of my neighbour's garage door were on and they stayed on. They don't usually do that. They are motion lights. Soon, in my mind, they were no longer lights on a garage--they were the eyes of God looking at me, reminding me that He could take my mistakes and use them for His purpose. Should I go on slap-dashedly making mistakes? God forbid! But while I was sleeping He was watching! "He will not let your foot slip – He who watches over you will not slumber..." Psalm 121 (NIV) Good news or what?

God wants us to FEEL HIS PRESENCE!

FB Post - Nov. 9, 2013

We had folks for supper last night. One couple we have known almost forever. The other, we barely knew. In fact, it was so "barely" that we were not even sure of their names. They had retired to our town, moved in next door to our friends and the remaining circumstances that brought us together are not important, except that I am reminded that they could have been part of our town for years and years without crossing our paths. Do these things happen for a reason? God's reason? I would like to think so. They came, we ate, we laughed, they shared stories of how God had worked in their lives, we had a few of our own. And I felt a "sweet, sweet Spirit in this place" – God's Spirit. I am so glad He came!

Back to those mice! I still haven't interviewed the farmer's wife. I still don't know why she didn't cut their heads off or if she cut the tails off all at once or in bits and pieces. In fact, I suddenly realize that I don't even know what the mice would lose with the loss of their tails. How important were those long, wiggling pencils that they dragged around behind them? Hmm! So I went to that great source of facts and figures, that seemingly limitless well of advice and instruction all hidden in a black box that I can carry under my arm, and found the following: a mouse's tail serves him in his locomotion and balance. It seems as if the lopping of the farmer's wife stopped the poor mice dead in their tracks, maybe knocked them off their feet, perhaps even stuck them down forever to that "bathroom counter" as a decoration. But who wants to gaze on a stuck down mouse!

Yes, we are quite like the three mice--working so hard to be comfortable that we miss seeing God, miss feeling His presence and consequently are plagued with blindness, spiritual blindness and thus we lose our "tails."

That, however, is not the end of the story. Though there are consequences that we will never be free of, just like the little mouse will never have his tail, and though Satan has tremendous power in our world, I believe that God has a characteristic that Satan can never attain. It is only God who can take a life without a "tail" and work in it to make it worthwhile and useful and blessed. Satan cannot do that!! I don't know what the theologians call this phenomenon. I call it grace!

Is this the reason for my "pit"? Am I here because I needed this "blackness", this "brokenness" to see God, to learn to feel His presence?

I had a visitor this afternoon. Her children are four, ranging in age from pre-teen to mid-teen. When it was evident that we had chatted too long for her to be home before they arrived from school, she relaxed and later called to let them know where she was. I heard bits of the conversation--on this end, "No, I cannot bring you a chocolate bar. I will not be near a store and you do not need a chocolate bar". A few more words and the conversation concluded. It was only a moment until her phone rang with another pleading for a chocolate bar. We expect this from the young, but I couldn't help but wonder how often I approach God in the same way. He must surely scratch His head and say, "Oh, my child, do you not know, have you not heard? There is no eternal filling in comfort. If there was I would not have had to die."

I hope I have not stretched the allegory too far, expected too much from those poor blind mice, but from their story I see that comfort will never be a way out of the "pit". In fact, when I go deep I see clearly that it is more likely to lead me further in.

So, I am left with my Bartimaeus eyes, with Jesus saying softly in my ear, "What do you want?" And I answer, "I want you, God." But how do I find Him!

CHAPTER 5

The pressure of my circumstance

MEDITATION - For God who said, "Let light shine out of darkness" made His light shine in our hearts to give us the light of the knowledge of the glory of God in the face of Christ. 2 Corinthians 4:6 (NIV)

Isaiah said that the Lord spoke to him "with a strong hand." Isaiah 8:11. Oswald Chambers (1963) calls this the pressure of our circumstance.

I have a new friend whose life, a number of years ago, was indeed impacted by "the pressure of her circumstance." She was a farmer's wife in a small Ontario town, the mother of three little boys, her life pretty much ordered by the daily demands of her situation. One morning her husband went to the barn to do the morning chores. When he returned to the house he found his wife blind. Their circumstances immediately changed, their faith and attitude toward God did not. They saw this situation as a message from God that would change their lives, though they knew not how.

I don't know the detail of how they moved from this small Ontario town to a tribal area of Senegal in Africa. I only know from the story that her husband told that they lived there for 39 years, that they never asked for a dime of support from anyone in all those years, that without medical training he did what he could to help the area sick, and without flight training he flew supplies in to the impoverished people that they lived among. He ended his story by telling us that the Lord had given him his wonderful wife for 49 years, but now He had asked for her back. He went on to tell us that his wife now had Alzheimer's and was a resident in the Long Term Care Centre where I visit weekly.

I have come to love this woman dearly. I often find her with a huge laundry basket of cloths--brown cloths, green cloths, gold cloths. She is carefully folding them, stacking them, unfolding them and folding them again and restacking them. All this is done with a quiet concentration and joyful smile. You see, the children will be along soon and will need dry cloths. Do I feel sorry for this woman? Not a bit! Sometimes I have to stretch my imagination to its limit to join her in her world, but it is always a world full of peace, of generosity, of gratitude for God's gifts. She is always glad that she was home when I came down her road, that there is a pie in the oven almost done and we will be able to share a cup of tea and a piece of pie in just a minute or so. There are clean sheets on the bed and if I would like I can spend the night. She has been praying for my boys (how did she know I had boys) and Jim has gone to help some folks, but he will be home any minute. I hold her hand and stroke her arm and wander through her world with her, a world so different from many--a world free of discontent, of criticism, of complaint. When I go to leave and give her a hug, she always takes my face in her hands and tells me she will pray for me; often she tells me I am an angel sent from God and she hopes that she is home the next time I come down her road.

Circumstances! Do we see God's hand in them moving us to places where He wants us to be, to attitudes He wants us to have? Or are they just happenings in our lives to us? This lady's muddled mind has done more to change my attitude toward what my life is than probably anything else over the 70-plus years of my journey. I am so thankful that He saw fit for me to know her

P.S. Don't ask me when or how, but somewhere along her journey her sight was restored.

I am not sure how long ago from today I first penned the above words. My friend has since passed away. In the time that I have known these people (and I have not known them well as to the daily details of their lives, but I feel that I have known their spirit), I have heard him say several things that will impact my thinking forever.

I heard him say of their situation when he returned from his chores to find his wife blind: "We sat at the kitchen table and decided that we had enough faith to die, but we didn't have enough to live."

We stood at my kitchen counter, with my writing down a new address and phone number of his, when suddenly he said, "Let's pray." Wouldn't you think that a man in his circumstance would have at least one request for God to make improvement in his circumstance? Not so!! He asked not for one thing. He thanked God for who He was, he thanked God for his wonderful wife and he thanked God for me. Never have I been so humbled. Never have I felt so filled. I am so thankful that God chose that our paths should cross. I am so thankful for the result of His goodness.

It was through that in-law process that I first knew a man who has become a dear friend. From him I first heard this concept--the concept that the value of any circumstance depends on through which lens I see it. If I view the circumstance as through a window and my eyes behold the great God of the universe, then the circumstance will become a tool through which God can work and it will have eternal value; but if I see the circumstance as one looking in a mirror then all I see is me and it becomes just one more contributing factor to my emptiness. Pain or pleasure can have the same result; either can be an addition to the great well of living water flowing from me because God's Spirit lives within or can add to the cesspool of stagnant water that makes its home in the well of my self-centeredness. The choice is mine.

How does God view our pain? How can I even begin to know the mind of God, His great infinite heart? I cannot. Perhaps, however, He has left us a hint or two. In 2

Chronicles 36:15 (NIV) it says: "The Lord, the God of their ancestors, sent word to them through His messengers again and again because He had pity on His people." Psalm 56:8 tells me that God cares enough about me that He stores up my tears in His bottle. (KJV)

The crowning indicator of how God feels about our pain is found in the very WORD OF GOD, leaving His rightful place of absolute perfection and coming to this earth which He had created to be a place of perfect beauty but which was then and still is spoiled beyond recognition by our acceptance of the lies of THE LETHAL LIAR. While here, He endured every pain, every pain in its nature, every pain in its intensity that we could ever be called to endure; but He went further than that: He took on pain that we have never been asked to endure. He took on Himself the pain of God turning His back, leaving Him all alone because of our acceptance of that LETHAL LIAR. Because He did, we can choose never to suffer that final pain. Who am I to view my pain as looking into a mirror and seeing only myself?

The company had all gone from the home of my friends; only we two remained behind. For what reason I cannot remember, but what followed has remained in my memory for more than 20 years. There was a table still laden with platters that had been full with desserts, and some still held quite a bit. Our hostess reached for a morsel to nibble on. I heard not a word but there must have been a look from her husband for I heard her say: "Matt, you cannot save me from myself."

Is that God's great mission in my life? To save me from myself? Is that why my pain is necessary? To save me from myself? Or might it even be that God is using me as His vessel to be a blessing to someone else? Then should I not be honoured that He trusts me to be a part for His work in another's life? Oh! The mystery! Do I trust God enough to leave it with Him?

My fingers are touching the keys, forming these words, one day before the first year anniversary of the massacre of twenty precious first graders in Newtown, Connecticut. Their parents, apparently, have asked all to do something good for someone else tomorrow in memory of their children. How full of God's grace is that? Would we not understand if their thoughts were full of cynicism, of bitterness that lessons that might have been learned from their tragedy have been lost to the consciousness of the many? Would we not understand if they yelled and screamed tomorrow at the injustices done to them by a broken world? Do they not have the right to demand their rights? But none of those is the stance of their grief! In their witness, I hear Jesus saying, "Father, forgive them for they know not what they do."

Watching this tragedy unfold a year ago broke my heart on many levels. One of those levels was how quickly the circumstance evolved into an argument regarding people's rights. It is Oswald Chambers in the book <u>My</u>

<u>Utmost For His Highest</u> who states unequivocally and without apology and over and over again throughout the book that God's first and foremost command to us is that we must give up our right to ourselves. It was from the soil of these thoughts that I wrote the following on Christmas day, 2012.

"Newtown"

'Tis Christmas morn and as I sit in my gown

My thoughts are awash with the folks of Newtown.

I can't even imagine their long, tear filled nights

While others around them just want their own rights.

I get a vision of the great cosmic war

And that the choices I make will alter the score.

Not on Google or Mapquest can the warzone be found.

The desires of our hearts make up the battleground.

Then I hear God's voice saying: "Child, try it My way.

For your right to do that a big price I did pay.

It started in a manger. It ended on a cross."

But we say: "Oh no! Of my life I'll be boss."

Then I hear Satan chuckle from somewhere below.

And I hear him say: "Why don't they know?

They make the same choices again and again.

It opens the door to send them more pain."

But over the noise of the guns and the brawl

If we listen closely we'll still hear His call.

Come unto Me. I will give you rest.

The world is in the midst of laying one man to rest today. The process will last several more days. He has the attention and the admiration of the world, not because he was rich or star-style famous, but rather because he cared about people and was willing to give of his self for them. Were the circumstances of his life easy and pretty? Would we ever view 27 years in a South African prison, a prison described to me by my South African friend as the Alcatraz of South Africa, as pretty? It would seem to me that this horrible, hurtful experience and his reaction to it helped to form the person that was able to, as the President of the United States put it, release not only the prisoner, but the jailor.

I quote the prisoner: "No one is born hating another person because of the color of his skin, or his background, or his religion. People must learn to hate, and if they can learn to hate, they can be taught to love, for love comes more naturally to the human heart than its opposite." (Mandela, 1994)

I had intended not to get into the deep waters of the subject of forgiveness, mostly because I feel totally unqualified, but I shared a thought that I had with a dear friend and she encouraged me to. So here I go into the deep waters. Here are a few thoughts I have had over the years.

1) Who do I hurt by my lack of forgiveness? Two people--the person who has hurt me and me. By not forgiving I fail to see the person as God sees that person; I fail to see the possibility inherent in that person to be better. I cut myself off from the chance to play a part in that journey to a better place. I fully realize that I must not be an enabler, that boundaries may need to be set. But those things don't interfere with forgiveness. They help it. I also hurt myself because an unforgiving heart festers into anger, hate and self-pity. An unforgiving heart keeps us from seeing God.

2) A different thought I had only recently. It is much easier to forgive an event than a person, easier to forgive what a person has done than who that person is by nature, day after day. The event fades

in our memory as time passes and so becomes easier to let go of, but the person remains the same. This becomes even more difficult if the person is someone we are not fond of in the first place. Sins we think we absolutely could not stomach take on a different hue when they are committed by someone we love. Could some of these be the reason God holds tight to His right to be the judge? Could this also be the reason that seemingly God has no trouble forgiving us over and over again-- because He loves us so much? Good news, right?

3) I think forgiveness has an elusive nature about it, that just when we think we have forgiven is probably just when we haven't. Could it be that forgiveness is not something we can analyze or argue about, something to be qualified and quantified but rather is part of our very nature? But it is only as we are filled with God's very nature that it becomes possible for us to forgive. These become scary thoughts when I lay them out on paper because I know from Scripture how much my forgiveness is tied to my forgiving others. It should send me back again to the lifelong task of knowing God so intimately that He can change me.

In the midst of writing this, I received the following from a dear sister-in-law on this wonderful modern invention called a computer: Joy sometimes needs pain to give it birth. Fanny Crosby could never have written her beautiful hymn, "I shall see Him face-to-face," had it not been for the fact that she had never looked upon the green fields nor the evening sunset nor the kindly twinkle in her mother's eye. It was the loss of her own vision that helped her to gain her remarkable spiritual discernment. (Cowman, 2006)

Circumstances!! What a mystery!!!

Our house sits on the side of a hill that slopes gradually from the street to the end of our back yard and then takes a steep climb to its rim. This phenomenon means that when this *never-to-have-made-five-feet* lady sits in my upstairs living room chair, by only lifting my gaze the slightest bit I look at the tops of the tall trees that populate our subdivision. My natural line of vision through my living room window takes in the roof line of the house across the way and sees easily the two motion lights on each side of the garage door. When I rise early in the morning and sit in my chair, darkness is often the most prevalent view that I have. Then, because something has moved somewhere close by, the lights come on. Then they go off. The most fascinating to me is when one of the lights pops on, then almost immediately goes off, and the one on the other side pops on. This rhythm of light often becomes a dance, back and forth, back and forth. My heart wants to know the reason for this dance. Is some animal moving that quickly back and forth or do even the tiniest ants, in their scurry, cause the sympathy of the lights and they turn on to show the little ant his way. Then my mind wanders to the *often darkness* of our circumstances. Is God watching us deal with the darkness and has sympathy for us and turns on a wee light of our understanding and we catch a glimpse of His great work in us? Is it so, though, that He cannot leave it on and in so doing destroy our chance of learning what we need to learn from the circumstance? Then, as we more and more look through the window of our circumstance and see God, our understanding increases, our love for Him flourishes and the lights come on for us and show us the way through whatever lies ahead...and we learn and we learn!

CHAPTER 6

With a passion

MEDITATION— "We are nearly always longing for an easy religion, easy to understand and easy to follow; a religion with no mystery, no insoluble problems, no snags; a religion that would allow us to escape from our miserable human condition; a religion in which contact with God spares us all strife, all uncertainty, all suffering and all doubt, in short, a religion without a cross. – Tournier

PASSION! There is that naughty word--almost always dripping with lust and licentiousness. Even between the covers of the Bible it seldom gets good press. But it is a good word, a God word! Six times, yes, even seven, in the first chapter of Genesis God looks at what He has done and the text renders it: God saw that it was good, even *very* good! Was this just an intellectual review of His work on God's part, notebook in hand, checking off the items as He came to them to make sure He had followed the pattern? Or did His great heart swell with passionate joy as He anticipated the beauty of the life that His creation could enjoy, filled with love, His love, in this beautiful home that He had created? Can you then, however, picture the broken-hearted passion that He must have felt when later the record shows that He repented that He had made man? What kind of passion must even now reside in that great heart for us that His focus in every action still sees the possibility in the love and the beauty if He can draw us back to His side?.

I love the story of the Samaritan woman in John 4. It is pregnant with mystery! It is pregnant with passion! The mystery shows itself at the very beginning of the story. "He had to go through Samaria." (John 4:4 NIV.) He did? I wonder how many Jews before Him had made their way from Judea to Galilee without the soles of their sandals touching Samaritan soil. In Verse 8: the disciples had gone into town to buy food. Hmmm! I wonder how much luck they had, how easy would it have been to find someone in a small Samaritan village, Sychar, who would serve this hot and hungry ragtag group of Jews. I am left with the mystery!

Meanwhile, back at the well, a Samaritan woman appears and Jesus deftly draws her into a discovery of her own passion. I wonder how many wanderers may have approached that well and turned and left in absolute amazement at what they saw--a Jewish man sharing in a conversation with a Samaritan woman. Unheard of! On many different levels! Did Jesus start right in cleaning up her life that He knew so well needed to be cleaned up? No, He simply asked her for a drink! This Word of God began the process of helping someone else by exposing His own vulnerability! Oh my! Oh my! How differently we want to work! How differently the Samaritan woman wanted to work. She wanted to deal with the obvious (you have no bucket), with her own comfort (give me this water so I don't have to keep coming here), with religion rather than her own emptiness (where should we worship). Jesus carefully and gently keeps drawing her back to her own need. The result is amazing, full of passion!!

FB Post -August 27, 2013

"It is in the dark struggles with God that we are surprised by His response to our anger and fear. What we receive from Him during our difficult battle is not what we expect. We assume He wants order, conformity – obedience. Instead, we find that He wants our passionate involvement and utter awe in the mystery of His glorious character." (Allender & Longman, 1999)

Even though Jesus had identified her problem to her, she was not ready to look at it. She reached for a way to put it off, deal with it later, for her answer to His probing comment was, "When the Messiah comes He will explain everything to us." Then the disciples returned from their shopping trip. It was at this point that her dialogue with Jesus must have trickled to the deepest recesses of her heart for she left the well and she returned to her village. She not only left the well, she left her bucket. I can't help but wonder when she realized what she had done. But her heart was so taken with what Jesus had told her that all she could think of was sharing this information with her fellow villagers. What must have been her demeanor, what must have been the passion in her voice to cause the citizens of Sychar to leave the tasks that they surely must have needed to do and go to the well to see who this man was? Why would anything this woman of ill repute had to say make any difference to the people of the town? But they did! And they have made a difference to me!

"Many of the Samaritans from that town believed on Him because of the woman's testimony, 'He told me everything that I ever did'." Wow! I have heard a few testimonies in my time, but they almost always start with the word "I". This one started with the word "He". Could it be that her time with Jesus refocused her thinking, her feelings away from herself and focused them on Him? Then, to make the episode more intriguing, these Samaritan Sychar citizens had the nerve to ask this Jewish Messiah to go home with them. And He did! He went and stayed two days! Where did He stay? Did the Samaritan woman go back to the home she had left when she went for water? Did she roll right back into the same bed she had rolled out of that morning? Can you just see the headline in the Sychar Sentinel the next morning? "Woman of Ill Repute Engages in Conversation with Jewish Man at Jacob's Well." The article might have gone on to say that this man was now in their town. It might have gone on to wonder if there would be dangerous repercussion from this episode between a Jewish man and a Samaritan woman of ill repute. These are the things that often start a war. This story, full of passion, has many ramifications for us. One is found in John 4:42 (NIV) where they said to the woman, "We no longer believe just because of what you have said...." Don't you wonder why this little bit of information is recorded in the Book of Books? Did they say it because they wanted to distance themselves from this neighbor who was an embarrassment to them? Or is it recorded to form a question that we all must answer? Passionately answer? I often wonder what I believe that I would actually be willing to die for? This goes all the way back to the second chapter in this book. Until the SONG is my own, until I have wrestled with God and answered the deep questions that relationship with Him dumps into my life, I am probably not doing much more than mimicking what someone else has told me. I hear the Psalmist in Psalms 25: 4 (NIV) passionately pleading: "Show me your ways, Lord, teach me Your paths."

Come with me now to John 20:11-17 (NIV). I love this accounting of the Resurrection story. Here we find Mary Magdalene, while others came and checked out the tomb and then left, standing outside with her broken heart, pouring out tears of deep emotion because His body was gone from the tomb and she knew not where. Was it this deep emotion that precipitated Jesus' choosing to appear to her first? Her love for Him was so deep, their relationship so close that a simple *Mary* from His voice brought recognition--she knew who He was. It was to her He entrusted the first *Good News:* "Go instead to my brothers and tell them I am ascending to my Father and your Father, to my God and your God." What a story! What a blessing! That same blessing, that same possibility of intimacy with the God of the universe, has been extended to me through Jesus' words to Mary--*my Father and your Father, my God and your God*. How could the beauty of this not stir a deep passion in us?

"But whatever you do, find the God-centered, Christ-exalting, Bible-saturated passion of your life, and find your way to say it and live for it and die for it. And you will make a difference that lasts. You will not waste your life." (Piper, 2003) There is a thought in Acts 26:16 (NIV) that I love. Paul is telling his story to King Agrippa when he recounts Jesus saying to him: ".....I have appeared to you to appoint you as a servant and as a witness *of what you have seen and will see of me.*" Wow!! Is my story so different? Am I not to be a servant and a witness of what I see in Jesus, of my relationship with God? Oh! I know--I have never seen that big light on the road to Damascus. I wouldn't even know how to find a road to Damascus. But I have seen God work on my own road, on my own journey. As I focus on God Himself, I am conscious of His presence more and more. I see Him in my little dog curled up asleep across the room from me; I see Him in the violets sitting in their spot in the room side of the north window, blooming and blooming and blooming, with just a wee sip of tea every three or four days to inspire them to put out one more bloom or two; I see Him in the ministrations of Husband as he works hard to fill the gap left by my unsightedness. God all around me, God in me convicting me of my failed humanity so often, God stretching far and beyond what my eye can see, what my ear can hear, what my mind can understand. But His Spirit, the great Spirit of God, bears witness with my spirit, my often lost, longing spirit, that I am His child. (Romans 8:16 NIV)

We have in our possession a CD entitled "316+". It is a compilation of 100 Bible passages read by 100 different voices – passages that stretch one to a greater zeal to want to journey deeper into the heart of God--voices that often stir up this zeal, this passion by their very cadence, indeed by the passion heard in that cadence. One voice touched me deeply. It was an old, quavering voice reading the 23rd Psalm. His voice put me in touch with the Shepherd because I could hear that he was in touch with the Shepherd. I felt the peace, the comfort of the *STILL WATERS* because I heard the peace and comfort in his voice. The quaver in the voice along with the passion told me that when he read "Yea, though I walk through the valley of the shadow of death" (KJV), it was something very real to his heart. We had not been in possession of the CD very long until I heard this man had passed away and I cried. His name I know not, his face I would not recognize; but because of his voice, because of what I heard in the voice, I love him. He has impacted my heart forever and I am thankful for the experience.

What do I want? I want to leave the wilderness of discouragement, dissatisfaction and disappointment and feel instead the *green pastures, the still waters, the table spread before me* of Psalm 23. I want that with a passion. And I have come to believe that God will honour that passion and will step by step save me from myself (no one else can), teach me the things I need to know in His way and in His time, and I will come to feel the peace that passes understanding that He so often promised. Oh! What a WONDERful way to live!

CHAPTER 7

Practice, Practice, Practice

MEDITATION: The story is told of a New York City tourist looking for Carnegie Hall. His first thought, when he encountered a young man carrying a violin was that this would surely be the person to direct him. So he stopped him and asked: "Could you tell me the way to Carnegie Hall?" The young man's answer: "Practice, Practice, Practice."

What do I want more than anything else? What is my passion? I tell myself I want to know God, find an intimacy with Him that will lead me to the peace that passes understanding that He promised, find the secret that will dispel the three big D's in my life: the D of discouragement, the D of dissatisfaction, the D of disappointment. Do you have a Big Three in your life that you struggle with? Then it seems to me the next question must be, AM I WILLING TO DO THE HARD WORK?

Sarah Young in her book <u>Jesus Calling</u> deals with this concept over and over again. A quick skim through her book looking for the word *practice* finds the following: *practice of listening to God, practice acknowledging God's sovereignty, practice trusting God, practice focusing on God in all of life's details, practice peace with God, practice gratitude to God, practice intimacy with God...PRACTICE, PRACTICE, PRACTICE.*

My daily journey in this book drew my thoughts one day to my grandson who is now in his third year in music at his chosen university. His primary discipline is Performance Piano. When he was in the final two years of his High School education, along with getting very good academic marks and holding down a part time job, he practiced his piano and studied his music four hours a day. This focus, this discipline earned him top marks in his country in one area of his study.

Romans 8:28 tells me that God works for the good of those who love him in all things. But how? By ridding me magically of the three D's? By turning every hard thing in my life into something soft and easy at the wink of an eye? For me, the answer lies in verse 29. He wants me to be conformed to the image of His Son--to the likeness of Jesus who gave up every right that He had to accomplish God's will for His life. I will not be conformed, however, if I resist His work in my life. Then what must I do to let Him? Could it be that I must practice, practice, practice? Am I willing to spend four hours a day in close proximity (Google tells me that a synonym for close proximity is a hair's breadth away), yea! only a hair's breadth from Him for Him to make me more like Jesus? I will go on to suggest that it is a 24/7 proposition. Oh dear!! How can this gargantuan task be accomplished? When I contemplated this, a verse quoted often by preachers of my youth wandered through my mind. I can hear them saying "Gird up the loins of your mind" and explaining what that meant, but I couldn't remember where it was. So I took my trusty Kindle, pressed a button to my trusty NIV version of the Bible, another button to Search This Book, typed in the word *GIRD* and pressed one more button expecting the search to be over. The result: zilch! The word was nowhere in the NIV. So I checked the NASB--same result. Surely those preachers from bygone years hadn't made it up. I then checked the older King James translation and there it was--1 Peter 1:13. So if you, dear reader, are under fifty, or maybe even sixty, this may be an unknown word to you. Newer translations render it *prepare yourself* or *be alert* but I am not sure those words carry the depth of meaning that *gird* does. In my searching I also ran across this expression: *gird them with girdles.* Oops! There is another word that the under fifties or sixties, I expect, know not of. But I do. I remember times, as a little girl, being hugged tight by a grandmother or great-aunt and feeling certain that the wall of the brick house had suddenly sprouted arms and held me firmly in its grip. The surface that I was being squeezed against was hard and firm, letting none of the rolling hills under its surface out for air. Those days are gone--the days of corsets and girdles; but God's concept is not. It is still important for us to practice the control of our minds, indeed, of our whole self and seek Him daily.

There isn't a lot in this world that I have control over--not the weather, not the politics of my country or town, not my deteriorating sight or my disappearing memory, not husband or child or church member or friend, and certainly not the length of my life. A simple exercise in basic arithmetic tells me that those remaining years cannot be many. Yet when and how they end I cannot control. He does, however, leave with me, I believe, the control of my mind, but that responsibility will only benefit me when I willingly turn even that back to God, when I, as Oswald Chambers says over and over again in his book <u>My Utmost for His Highest</u>, *I must give up my right to myself.* Only then will the big 3D's dissipate.

FB Post - Oct. 8, 2013

I was thinking just now of my bank--thinking that I would need to call them for help with something, thinking how the nice lady I deal with gave me her card that lets me call her directly. That led me to think about how I am, increasingly, willing to pay more for a product if I can buy it where someone will help me. I need that help because I have a disability: I cannot see well. Most folks are willing to look for the cheapest, quickest way of getting done what needs to be done because they "can do it by themselves". Is there a spiritual lesson to be had here? Could it be that Satan moves right in and encourages us to solve the problems of our lives by ourselves? Could it be that it takes the big jolts in life that we can no longer fix by ourselves before we can admit our neediness, our brokenness and God moves in and does His majestic, mysterious work? I am thankful for His work.

Are you of an age that you experienced the school time discipline of writing lines over and over--fifty times the same words, a hundred times the same words? Mine were almost always the same and contained the word *talking*.

I have a dear friend who experienced her own time of brokenness and who found her own unique way of practicing the presence of God in her life. She has graciously shared her experience with you here and I thank her.

My Healing Process

In the early 1970's I had what is called a "nervous breakdown". I don't think that is an accurate explanation but I'm not sure what else to call it. This deep darkness (depression) just wouldn't let up. I felt like the devil had gripped me and I couldn't get away. I would ask my husband if he thought I would ever be well again. He always assured me I would but the days, months and years dragged on. I felt numb. I didn't know how to draw on what had been my faith. That too had disappeared. The doctors gave up on me because I couldn't take the drugs they offered. They sent me home saying that my husband would have to take care of me.

One night when I couldn't sleep, I picked up a bible that was on the night-stand next to our bed. I randomly opened it and it fell on Exodus chapter 3 where it talks of Moses and the burning bush. Verse 14(b) says; "This is what you are to say to the Israelites: I AM has sent me to you".

That passage kindled a spark in me, so I asked myself if God is I AM and obviously Jesus knows his I AM because many scriptures tell us that Jesus referred to himself by saying I AM the Way, the Truth and the Light, the salt of the earth, the bread of life, etc. etc. So what then is my I AM??

From this came my decision to create my own identity (I AM) from the scriptures. I began with Galatians 5: 22 & 23. I read the fruit of the Spirit over and over again. Then I decided to write each fruit individually saying; "I AM love, I AM joy, I AM peace, I AM patience, I AM kindness, I AM goodness, I AM self-control. I chose one fruit per day and wrote it over and over repeating it to myself, putting emphasis on each word, (I am love, I AM love, I am LOVE). As I wrote I asked myself how it felt to be Love. How would others feel if I were Love? How do I express Love? How do I feel when others show Love to me? I did this for several months every day, taking each word and calling it my I AM. I looked at 1 Corinthians 13:4-8 and created I AMs from there. I looked at Philippians 4:8 where it told me to "think on these things". I would keep my mind focused on whatever was good, kind, etc. Lastly I studied the Beatitudes. I realized they are not HAVE-attitudes, they are BE-attitudes. So I needed to look at myself and see if I really was poor in spirit, mournful, meek, etc. etc. These also became part of my "I AMs".

Finally after many, many months of working my I AMs the dark cloud lifted and I felt closer to God and His Son than I ever had before. But I also know I must keep them active in my life each day, even now, so I repeat some I AMs as I go about my every day duties. I also find it very helpful to daily repeat what I call my mantra: "I Act in Faith and I let go of all Fear. I Live in Hope and I let go of all Doubt. I Serve in Love and I let go of all Anger. Therefore I am at peace both within and without".

My friend knows, on a personal level, the meaning of practice, practice, practice.

Acts 17:16 begins with these words: "Now while Paul was waiting for them at Athens." (NASB). We do lots of that, don't we? As Paul waited he took a walk around the city to see what he could see. What he saw saddened him--idolatrous gods everywhere. And just to be sure they had their backs covered, the Athenians had erected a god they called "the unknown god". It didn't take long for circumstances to develop so that Paul found himself addressing the Athenian philosophers. A chance meeting? I don't think so! Paul says several very meaty things in the course of this discourse that we would do well to ponder, but the phrase I love is this: "...that they would seek God, if perhaps they might *grope* for Him and find Him...." (Verse 27, NASB). *Grope* is not a pretty word in our culture, but then it meant "search blindly or uncertainly by feeling with the hands" (Oxford Dictionary). I know what it is to grope! I know what it is for my sight to fail and I find myself groping to find a door. I know what it is to lean over my kitchen counter and swipe its surface with my whole arm from my elbow to my wrist, trying to find some elusive spoon or bottle cap that I have laid down only moments before. Groping doesn't do a lot to add to a feeling of personal importance. Groping does do a lot to add to our feeling of need, of helplessness. We are not the same, but we are all blind, helpless humans. For our life to work, we need to find God. We need to learn to practice, practice, practice something that will lead us ever closer to Him. For Ann Voskamp, it was learning gratitude by counting gifts. Husband is trying her plan. He is at gift number 494. For Sarah Young, it was arming herself with Bible, notepad and pen every morning and making her way to her special spot and spending time with God. For me, my feet need to hit the floor every morning sometime between 4:00 and 5:00 AM. That allows me at least two hours and maybe three before life starts to happen at my house. For more than fifteen years I have spent that time in reading <u>My Utmost For His Highest</u> by Oswald Chambers. As time has gone by, I have added <u>Jesus Calling</u> by Sarah Young and then a reading and re-reading of Louis Giglio's book, <u>Worship: The Air I Breathe</u>. I read this because I want to be reminded daily that my life is my worship. I am still so filled with "self" that I mess up most days, but I am trying. What about the Bible, you say? I go there, too. The point is not how we practice being in the presence of God, but how often. We also need to be honest with ourselves as to why we want to do this. If our goal is simply to prove our rightness or righteousness, the darkness will not dissipate. I want to feel God, to sense God, to love God and feel His love for me. Paul went on to share with the Athenians that He is not far from any one of us, not even a hair's breadth away. While we are living life in the darkness of doubt, in the darkness of pain, in the darkness of self-centeredness or self-pity, He is right there beside us, wanting to help us fix it. But He can't do it if we don't know Him, trust Him, honour Him, love Him. It takes practice to see Him in the details of our lives 24/7.

"Morning Musings"

'Tis very early in the morning. The clock said four-thirty eight.

But my mind was already busy. Sleep had gone right out the gate.

My mind was full of great-grandchildren who have woven their way through my heart.

And to God I feel so thankful. How better my day to start?

Way up north there is Bayleigh so tall - already in Grade Two.

Next come sisters Maddie and Shiloh. Great Grandma can't tell who's who.

And staying at home with Mommy is Peyton. I call her Miss Peeps.

Her job is to take care of Mommy. From loneliness her Mommy she keeps.

And down in Southern Ontario, on Nana's floor cousins play.

Their names are Damon and Ella and Ella's sister is on the way.

So I go through the fabric left over from quilts made in days of yore.

And decide to make some wee quilts but I don't know how many more.

I could sit and muse forever on His wonderful gifts from above.

But I guess I best get busy and stitch in some stitches of love.

CHAPTER 8

Humility or Humiliation

MEDITATION: The righteous cry out, and the Lord hears them; He delivers them from all their troubles.

The Lord is close to the brokenhearted and saves those who are crushed in spirit. Psalm 34:17-18 (NIV).

"I have been driven many times upon my knees by the overwhelming conviction that I had nowhere else to go. My own wisdom and that of all about me seemed insufficient for that day." — Abraham Lincoln

It is January 30, 2014. Our little town is socked in with snow. Schools have been closed for days. I just pushed all the right buttons on my Kindle to purchase a new book, Prepared for A Purpose by Antoinette Tuff, a book whose publishing date is January 21, 2014. Of course, I have not read the book, but I have watched parts of her story unfold on TV. Could it be that the foundation of humility is worded perfectly in the title of this book? Is it possible that the soil in which humility grows is the conviction that every detail of our life is there as preparation for His purpose? Just wondering!

I am not a theologian, only a little person born female making my way down the pathway of life on this earth like millions of others, but I am also wondering if anger is not the most prevalent, the most prominent, the most deluding, the most debilitating emotion that any of us deals with. It manifests itself in different ways in us: with some, in our tear; with some, in our laughter; with some, it flows through the tips of our fingers; with some, in bursts as destructive as a major earthquake. The reason for our anger, however, is the same in each of us. We are unhappy with our lot in life. When anger wins, our passion for God Himself subsides, our determination to practice His principles wanes, our circumstances become front and center in our focus, self-pity sets in and anger has a fertile soil in which to multiply and mess us up; but if the above premise is true, if we are being prepared day by day, bit by bit for a purpose that we know not, and if we embrace that thought and make it a part of who we are, then would not the anger dissipate? Even those times when the life result is the product of our own sin, from the times that Satan has reigned supreme and we have fallen on our face, will not humility, if it is at work in us, help us to deal with that from God's perspective, not our own? *PREPARED FOR HIS PURPOSE* – what a beautiful thought! The purpose, however, must be God's, never my own, and that will send me to swim in the deep, deep pool of humility. When I find myself battling the tides of life, wanting to be in warmer waters, it is a sure sign I have not found His purpose, and my journey to the very heart of God will be impeded.

FB Post - August 1, 2013

"That's why your perspective is so valuable--you have fought for it and struggled intellectually and emotionally for the ground you hold." (Phillips, 2012) Oh, that we would listen to God Himself in the midst of our struggle, in the midst of our pain and instead of running from it, instead of blaming someone else for it, learn what He is trying to teach us. We can be of no earthly good to anyone else unless we do.

"The real question is: how can I live so that my death will be fruitful for others?" (Nouwen, 2001)

It is 3:27 AM, February 12, 2014. I have left my bed after lying there for more than two hours, thinking about the man called Brother Lawrence. A friend gave us this book more than ten years ago, and I read it then but without the haunting that it is creating in me now. Except that HIS book it was not. He didn't write a book, but his story lives on. I went to the man with the answer to all questions, Mr. Wikipedia, and found that Brother Lawrence was born Nicolas Herman in 1614 in France. 1614? What day, Mr. Wikipedia, what day? It seems he doesn't know. Nor, apparently, does anyone else. Yet, here I am in 2014 reading a book called <u>Practicing The Presence Of God</u> that has been republished on May 21, 2008, is Text to Speech Enabled, and was delivered to my Kindle via Amazon Whisperer. He died on February 12, 1691. That is 323 years ago today, if my arithmetic is correct, and all of this I only realized just now. Is that why I was awake so early? Did God intend for this man of so long ago to impact my life in yet another way today?

Matthew 5:5 (NIV) tells me this: "Blessed are the meek, for they shall inherit the earth." Who are these people, anyway? You will know when you meet one! But what does it mean they will inherit the earth? I expect I could find more than one interpretation of what this means if I searched, but which one would be right? I only know that this man known as Brother Lawrence with his wisdom and deep spirituality has begun to "inherit" my earth some 323 years later. And he never wrote a book. The book I read is a compilation of conversations people had with him, notes that were found after his death and letters that he wrote to people; but may I quote Mr. Wikipedia to give you just a wee glimpse of the magnitude found in his meekness.

"He spent almost all of the rest of his life within the walls of the priory, working in the kitchen for most of his life and as a repairer of sandals in his later years. Despite his lowly position in life and the priory, his character attracted many to him. He had a reputation for experiencing profound peace and visitors came to seek spiritual guidance from him. The wisdom he passed on to them, in conversations and in letters, would later become the basis for the book, *The Practice of the Presence of God*. Father Joseph de Beaufort."

It is interesting to me that Nicolas Herman was, at one point, the footman for the Treasurer of the King of France. He left that position because he was clumsy and awkward, always breaking things. Would I know anything at all about him 323 years later if he had remained in that position? You decide.

FB Post -September 8, 2013

As I sit in my chair, lumpy with age, in my familiar room my world is pretty small. But even in the small town in which I live, apparently the second safest place in all of Canada in which to live, a battle is going on concerning the use of some public buildings, with each side, I am sure, believing they are right and the other wrong. Across the greater world, high level meetings are being held to decide what weapons will be used and when to use them to lift up right and get rid of wrong. We "stand our ground" and fight for our concept of "right" at every level--in our homes, in our churches and schools, in every facet of our lives. Into the fray comes a loud and thunderous voice, and if we would listen we would hear Him say: "Can you make a mountain? Can you tame the wildest animals of the jungle and they will lie at your feet?" And in an instant that thunderous voice becomes a baby born in a dirty stable, a homeless, wandering man never demanding His rights. Then He is gone, leaving the Spirit of the thunderous voice, the Spirit of the homeless man to help us sort it all out, to help us be the peace we need in our homes, in our churches, in our schools, in our world, yea in our own hearts in order to make alive His message of peace, of selflessness, of service for another's good.

Aunt Emma's Funeral Eulogy

I don't know if there are any staff members here today or not, but we would be remiss if we did not laud them for their tender care of Aunt Emma. I have spent the night on the floor in my mother's room when she was ill, I have stayed the night in Aunt Emma's room, and on both occasions when staff would have no way of knowing whether I was asleep or awake, I have witnessed tender care. I listened the one night while two of the staff were turning and washing Aunt Emma. I heard their tender conversation with her as they worked even though Aunt Emma was unable to respond and as they finished one nurse leaned close to Aunt Emma's ear and said, "Oh, Emma, you are such a pet." There isn't a paycheck large enough to pay for that kind of devotion and I thank them for it.

The night before Aunt Gladys's funeral we stayed with friends. My host was always an early riser, so when I awoke very early in the morning, I knew that both coffee and television would be on. When I wandered out, the television was showing a memorial service for the Queen Mother, Elizabeth. She was described at that time as a woman of dignity, courage and laughter. I am not sure when along the time line between then and now that the seed germinated in my mind that those same words describing the Queen Mother perfectly fit my estimation of Aunt Emma, but I believe they do. Aunt Emma lived her life with dignity when under similar circumstances most of us would not have. So many things that most of us take for granted, Aunt Emma never had or did. She never had her own home, probably few if any of her clothes she got to pick out, and if she ever went shopping it was seldom. Just a few days before her stroke, as I was feeding her, I admired something she was wearing. I asked her where she got it, and first there came that endearing turn of the head and then, "I don't know. I guess somebody gave it to me." Uncle Mervyn described Aunt Emma to me as a work-horse. But seldom was it her own work; rather, it was work for others. She did it all with dignity and cheerfulness, and for the years that I knew her best, I felt nothing but love for those she was working for. Another time, just a few days before her stroke, as I was feeding her, Aunt Emma said to me, "Gladys always worked too hard. She just worked too hard." Just another indication that her thoughts were not for herself. Perhaps some may think that Aunt Emma was better able to accept life as it came to her than the rest of us would because she was a little slow. Those of us who knew her best know better. How many of you here would know my birthday? My husband and children sometimes have trouble with that. It was on my 67th birthday that Aunt Emma came into my Mother's room to inform her that "this is Wilma's birthday." I am not special. She would know this about everyone's life around her, and when one is a part of the clan that I was born into, those around her were many. Was Aunt Emma a victim? A victim of others, a victim of the times in which she lived, a victim of circumstances? Lots of folks would say yes, but if you asked Aunt Emma, she would laugh at you. Aunt Emma was never a victim, because her life was not about herself but about others; and she walked every step of that life with dignity.

Her life was courageous. Aunt Emma was born on March 5, 1911. When she was just two, a childhood disease impaired her hearing, affected her speech and her sight. In later years she would lose one eye; but Aunt Emma could do the most beautiful embroidery and crocheting one could imagine. No one begins or completes difficult projects such as these without some spunk. I have in my possession many things made by Aunt Emma--embroidered pillow cases, crocheted doilies, etc.--that will be a part of the cherished memory I have of her in the years to come.

Have you ever moved? How far did you move? As one who has moved often I know that it can be a difficult transition, sometimes hard to fit in to a new community, a new church and so on. What must it have been like for Aunt Emma in 1973 when she was 62 years old to move from her quiet northern Ontario community where she had been all her life to the middle of Toronto, to an address on Lawrence Avenue, one of the busiest streets in the city? She did it with courage. I know because I was there. I saw her fit right in and help Aunt Gladys with whatever there was to be done. I saw her take her place in the church as if that was where she had always been. Those kinds of transitions cannot be accomplished without courage.

And then there was the laughter...oh, the precious laughter. It was always so much fun to say something absolutely ridiculous in Aunt Emma's ear, to see that little cock of the head and then to hear those giggles bubble forth. One of those fun times came for me in Toronto when we were visiting Aunt Gladys and Aunt Emma. My husband asked

Aunt Emma if she would do something for him. She said she would, so he asked her if she would knit him a sock. You could see the puzzlement, then the mirth spread over her face. It said, "Why would anyone with two feet want one sock?" He then went on to say that he wanted it big enough to go over both feet. That is when the giggles started as she imagined what this creation would look like. Those giggles went on for quite a while, but the sock was made to fit over both feet. It is much easier to keep feet warm on a winter camp-out sleep if they are in one sock together. We still have that red sock.

She, indeed, was a woman of dignity, courage and laughter--in my estimation a queen. So, I can joyfully let her go to her Creator who loves her perfectly when we were often not able to. I know she is where she has her very own place deeded to her by none other than the Savior himself. The down payment was paid with her simple acceptance of the Savior's love for her, the mortgage payments made with her continuing commitment to that love manifested in her devotion to doing to the best of her ability what she believed was right.

And now she has her very own place and what is more, it is a mansion.

With a few adaptations, the above are the words that I spoke at my Aunt Emma's funeral. Her life was filled with humility. Humiliation – not so much!

FB Post - July 11,2013

We picked up Aunt Emma's chest of drawers from the furniture refinisher yesterday. Why I acquired Aunt Emma's piece when Aunt Emma left this earth I don't know, but it has sat for several years in the corner of my sewing nook, filled to the top with quilt related scraps and tools. The outside was marred somewhat by scratches and stains, but when I unpacked it for its trip for regeneration, I found that the drawers were cedar lined, a representation of its quality--and I was reminded of Aunt Emma. You see, Aunt Emma had been "marred" by earth's standards, but on the inside she was "lined" with qualities of greatness--with selflessness, with humour, with industriousness, with concern for others and with kindness. Qualities that caused the nurse charged with her care at the end of her life to bend over her and quietly say into her deaf and comatose ear, "Oh, Emma, you are such a pet."

I can think of nothing that would be more wonderful than for the greatest doctor of all time, that most perfect of nurses to whisper in my ear at the time of my last breath on this earth, "Oh, Wilma, you are such a pet." If humility is where I need to go to hear that, why would I not want to go there?

"But the plans of the Lord stand firm forever, the purposes of His heart through all generations. Blessed is the nation whose God is the Lord." Psalm 33:11-12 (NIV)

That great heart still beats strong for you and me!

CHAPTER 9

God on a train

MEDITATION:

You have searched me, Lord and know me.

Your majesty I surely believe.

You know when I sit and rise.

Your mystery I perceive.

But it's your mercy, daily mercy

That simply lets me breathe.

It happened on the train somewhere between Jasper, Alberta and Vancouver, British Columbia. We were riding the rails across our vast country. No, we weren't hobos riding the rails. We were paying participants along with many others from all over the world, enjoying this most unique of experiences. We were treated royally on this excursion. We were served our meals in a linen-laced dining car on a linen-covered table impeccably set and served by a maitre d' with his spotless white napkin folded over his arm which he never dropped, whether serving our soup or pouring our tea. Friendly, he was, and gracious in every possible way.

We had gone to the observation car to enjoy the ride through the Rocky Mountains and were so engaged when the train stopped dead on the tracks. The train had stopped many times on our trek across the country, usually in the dark of night. There would be much clatter and clanging in the dark as the train moved a little and then moved back to its original position, or so it seemed; but on this stop there was no clanging, no moving, only an eerie silence in our car, even though there were a number of people there for the same reason we were.

It wasn't long until I realized, from my westward wending seat by the window on the south side of the train, if I let my gaze drift to the forward right there were four or five beautiful mountains in my view. Some were taller than their brothers, they all stretched as high in the sky as they could, reaching with all their might for something just beyond their grasp. A couple of them had donned pure, white toques to protect their pointed heads from the chilly, September air. As I looked, I was reminded of Jesus' promise that if I had faith as a mustard seed I could move one of these mountains, and I wondered why I would want to They seemed perfect, so beautiful with their purple and pinkish hues dappling the scene from my train seat.

I began to wonder what life was like in the nooks and crannies of those mountains. Oh, I know--climbers have climbed mountains and claimed the highest peaks, but do they know of every bug and beetle making its home, living its life, raising its family in the deep, dark crevices that are up and down the sides of those mountains? God does, but perhaps only He. What about the comings and goings of the bison and the black bear, the mountain lion and the mountain goat, the pika and the prairie dog--all at home on the slippery slopes of these mountains with no one to monitor their daily activities except maybe the cawing crow or the foraging buzzard? Oh, what mysteries are hidden in the massiveness of those mountains.

However, I could not stay here any longer. My curiosity took me to the scene to my left, directly out the window from where I was sitting. What a sad, swampy scene it was. A gully stretched out for as far as I could see. Tall grasses grew up, twisted and tangled around each other, yearning for someone to come and untangle the uncomfortable mess they had become. Trees grew up throughout their habitat, standing tall like faceless ghosts with no garment to protect them from the tunnel winds riding up and down that gully. Their arms stretched out, ending in claw-like hands as if beseeching someone to come and feed the soil that was their home so that they could take on the same beauty as their brothers and sisters fortunate enough to live in a better place. I don't know why, but something made me press my face tight to the window and look as straight down the side of the train as I could to see what was there. I was amazed and dumbfounded. Along close to the edge of the tracks were three pools of colour--a red pool, a pinkish pool and a yellow pool. Wildflowers!! They could be tended by none other than the hand of God. And the tears came. They came because I felt so certain that I was, at that moment, witnessing the very essence of the nature of God. I was witnessing His Majesty, His Mystery and His Mercy. My thinking has ever been changed by that experience. The days I hold this concept close to me and let it carve out my day, it is a good day. The days I leave it behind and go on my way are never so good.

FB Post -September 7, 2013

My friend, Don Smith, used a phrase in his yesterday's post that I love--"God came near time." From now on that is what I am calling my 5 am to 7 am time. And so I sit in my chair, on a cool morning in my flannel nightie with my warm "Bryce" socks on, no one in the room seemingly except me and Remington. I may be on a page of the Bible, contemplating the thoughts of some author, cherishing in my mind the picture of a precious great-grandchild, contemplating the problem of a failed garden or on and on...and suddenly God is there with a profound message from the page of the Bible, or the mind of the author, or an overwhelming warmness from the picture of family, or a great lesson from some daily failure. "And He sits with me, and He talks with me, and He tells me I am His own"...and more and more that message is stretching beyond my "God came near time" into the activities and the relationships of the day and bringing peace and meaning to each event. I am thankful.

The most important relationship in our life, and for many of us, perhaps, the longest, is our relationship with God. A recognition with awe and wonder of His Majesty, a grateful acceptance of His Mystery without having to know how or why, and an emotion wrenching realization of His Mercy and what that means for our daily walk in life have helped me find a deeper peace in my relationship with Him. I still have a long way to go.

His majesty? What can I say? If I am really to wrestle with this question, I must start with a deep self-analysis of who MY God really is in relation to who I really am. Have I molded Him and made Him into a god that I can understand, handle, who doesn't challenge me too much to go beyond where I want to be? Or am I willing to throw myself out there (wherever that turns out to be) and let Him lead me, guide me, do with my life whatever He will? Tough question!

Here are just a few things I found in a very early morning journey with Mr. Google and Mr. Wikipedia into the Majesty of God: 1) The Milky Way (Louis Giglio calls this our subdivision) is a barred spiral galaxy some 100,000-120,000 light-years in diameter which contains 100-400 billion stars; 2) A light-year is the distance that light travels in a vacuum in one Julian year; 3) A light-year = 9460730472580800 metres (exactly) = 5878625 million miles. In contrast to these astronomical figures, later today a gentleman will come to my door, tape measure in hand, to measure the size of the three bedrooms that are a part of our house in order for him to know how much of the carpet that I have chosen will be needed to cover the floors of those three rooms. The tape will give him an answer--a few feet. As a believer in God, I love to ooh and aah over the first set of numbers; but where does my heart really live?

Am I willing to look deeply into every aspect of His Majesty? Will I stay and search out His Majesty very long in Revelation 3: 15-16 (NIV) which says: "I know your deeds, that you are neither cold nor hot. I wish you were either one or the other! So, because you are lukewarm--neither hot nor cold--I am about to spit you out of my mouth." (Some versions have the audacity to use the word "vomit".) This is not a pretty picture, but God is not always pretty. He is always just and He is always loving. His one concern is to draw us back to Himself. Who am I to question His ways? If I really internalize that, then why do I run from Him, try to explain away the many times that I am commanded to "Fear God"? If I truly come to understand His Majesty, will that not be part of the natural response to that Majesty? Parse it, explain it, theologize about it all we want, but in the end, if I am to get anywhere in this life-journey, I must come to grips with all those Omnis and they are all contained in that one word--Majesty!!

Then there is the Mystery!! Do you wonder about God, and if you do, does that uncertainty make you love Him more or less? Am I one of the people afraid to look beyond what I have always been taught, or am I one who has looked beyond and none of it made sense, so I have turned my back on God completely? I love words, the way they, when strung together, are so rich in meaning. Just such a stringing occurs in 1 Timothy 3:16 (NIV): "Beyond all question, the *mystery* from which true godliness springs is great." So much is so mysterious, makes no sense when looked at through the lens of our humanity. Let me tackle just one. In Acts 20:35 (NIV) Paul says this: "... we must help the weak, remembering the words of the Lord Jesus himself who said: 'It is more blessed to give than to receive.'" What? What sense does that make in our way of thinking? Yet it works every time! It doesn't matter whether we are talking about the big bucks or the price of a cup of coffee, whether we are talking about ten minutes of our time a week, next Tuesday, or a lifetime in some foreign land. What God can do with it depends on the heart inside us.

"Norman thanks you"

Last Saturday night I was at the "Building for Tomorrow" banquet for YFC/Youth Unlimited, Woodstock. I had the privilege of meeting Norman. He is a marvelous boy who has discovered our Open Sky Bike Co-op Ministry in downtown Woodstock, and Norman has become a regular fixture at the shop.

If you have seen the movie Forest Gump, Norman makes me think of Forest at age 13. He talks slowly, deliberately, and has a heart of gold; but just like the character Tom Hanks played in the movie, Norman's life has had more of its share of hardships and brokenness. Norman has a learning disability and is physically small for his age, making him a target of teasing and bullying. His father died a few years ago, and up until recently, he had no positive, caring male role model in his life. His hurt and sorrow would be expressed in temper tantrums and outbursts of frustration, a challenge to both his Mom and the educational system.

It is wonderful to see what difference a caring adult in a caring context can make in a young person's life. His mother says that the change in Norman has been amazing because of the daily interactions at the bike shop. Just like bicycles find new life at the co-op, so do people.

The above was written by my son, who has worked with YFC for more than twenty years. The gentleman responsible for the Co-op Bicycle Shop I do not know and, in respect of his privacy, will not name. I do know from his bio that he has every reason to be proud of his own personal accomplishments. Why would he spend his time in a bicycle shop? What reward is there for him in that? The mystery! It is more blessed to give than receive. A part of God--God the Father and God in the flesh. A part of the mystery that, if practiced, works every time-- always has, always will. As one old man said once, "If you haven't tried it, you are in no position to argue." Far more joy will come from this mysterious God-principle than will ever come from new carpet on three bedroom floors.

Now we come to His mercy! Oh My! The Bible says He numbers even the hairs of my head. Does He know the ones that have turned gray in the last few years? Or how many fell out in my brush just this morning? What does He do with all this information? Can He use it in some way to help someone else? I don't know the answer to all of these questions, but in just thinking about them, I am reminded of how much He cares for me. Were it not for His mercy, how could He love me?

When I went to my NIV Bible in my Kindle, typed in the word *mercy* in Search This Book, I was a little surprised to find almost every entry was in the form of a plea: "have mercy on me"; "be merciful unto me". David uttered this plea in one form or another over and over in the Psalms. Is that what is wrong with our world? Knowledge and wealth, convenience and ease have become so accessible to us that we have forgotten our need--we think we can do it by ourselves. Is that why angst lives so close to the surface? Could it be that it will only be when I really embrace my deep need for God's mercy that I will have the tools that I need to catch a glimpse of God's glory around me and in me, to appreciate His image in myself? Is that what gave Bill and Gloria Gaither the inspiration to write "Because He lives, I can face tomorrow. Because He lives all fear is gone"? What? ALL FEAR! Does the acceptance of this great Mercy then allow me to look deeply enough into the eyes of another to see a promise--a promise of possibility because that person carries within, no matter how covered by sin it might be, a little of the image of God? Instead of seeing a causer of the next big catastrophe, I see, rather, the causer of a little colour along the track of life; and I can help cause that colour, maybe with a handshake or a hug, maybe with a meal or a moment of my time. Colour to brighten another's life, mercy given passed on. A better world begins with me.

FB Post – March 2, 2014

I just connected with my FB after being away for seven days. My eyes first fell on a post by Don Smith where he used the precious word "precious" several times. This sent my mind on a backward trajectory over my past seven days--sailing in the Caribbean with the Gaithers. There were people there from all over--Norway, Sweden, South Africa, Brazil, England, Scotland, Australia, Canada, and, of course, the U.S.--and likely others. Precious! Here we were, different faith backgrounds, different political views, different climates, etc., but at the end of each day, we raised our voices with the professional musicians in praise to our shared precious God, we shared precious stories with each other, and many offered precious kindness to me because I was carrying a white cane. We were served by precious people with their own stories: a very, young man who had done this for six years and for a little of the year got to go home to Indonesia and be with his Mom and Dad; a newly married man from the Philippines, who for ten months of the year worked on the seas and for just two months got to go home and be with his bride, who was running her own business in her homeland. Yes, they picked up my dishes, brought me some coffee, but more importantly, they served me with their story; helped me to understand how big God is and that there are far more precious people in His love than me, my family, my church, etc. Precious People!

CHAPTER 10

God in His Majesty

MEDITATION: A better question becomes "Why does it matter?" It is not your responsibility to explain what God is doing with your life. He has not provided enough information for you to figure it out. Instead, you are asked to turn loose and let God be God. Therein lies the secret to the peace that transcends understanding. (Dobson, 2012).

Majesty! How do I get a glimpse of the majesty of God? Or is it everywhere around me and deep within me, but I fail to look and see? In Psalm 46:10 we have these words: He says, "Be still and know that I am God; *I will be exalted among the nations, I will be exalted in the earth.*" *(*NIV) [emphasis mine]. It is not hard to hear the first part of this verse quoted; it often is; but the last part not so much! This quote obviously comes from the pages of the Bible, but we don't even need to go there to know the truth of the last part of the statement. I was so saddened at Christmas time this last year to hear a historian, at the end of a documentary about Jesus, make the statement that Jesus feet had only just left the earth, when the power struggle began. How many nations over the course of history, how many churches, how many leaders, how many simple folk like me, have fallen and, in some cases, disappeared from the earth because the focus was self rather than a bowed spirit before the majesty of God? It was Sorenson Kierkegaard who said: "**Everyone whose life does not bring relative catastrophe has never even once turned . . . to God**, it is just as impossible as it is to touch the conductor of a generator without getting a shock." (Crabb, 2010). Is that what I really want from the great conductor of the Universe? Am I willing to recognize His Majesty if that is where it takes me?

FB Post July 10, 2013

We had folks for afternoon tea yesterday. They retired to our small town three years ago anticipating enjoying many years in this community. That dream has been interrupted by the march of Alzheimer's through the mind of the wife. I learned a lot about her yesterday from her own lips--that she was raised in Montreal, that she had two brothers who played hockey and she loved to go and watch, that she has a daughter who occupies many of her thoughts, that her favourite pie is pumpkin. I watched as her husband helped her find the path in her mind that she was searching to go down, who helped her identify the person at the end of the path, always in kindness and gentleness, all the while calling her dear. How does God's purpose in the world fit in to this kind of circumstance? I don't know. Should I pray that the difficulties they are experiencing be removed from their lives? I don't know. I only know that I felt the presence of God yesterday in our encounter with these folks we barely knew. When we parted, she and I hugged with the promise that we would get together again soon. For pumpkin pie!

I have long been fascinated with the story of Job in the Bible. Though it certainly speaks loudly to the mystery of God, it is saturated with glimpses of His majesty. We are told in the beginning of the story that Job was a rich man, a man above reproach. In the text he is called blameless and upright. It seems to me that blamelessness would be an almost impossible attribute to attain, right up there with the nature of God. He is described as the greatest man among all the people of the East. One day the angels appeared before God and Satan came with them. What Satan was doing hobnobbing with a group of angels, I can't imagine, but God's question to him was what he thought of His servant, Job. Satan's answer was quick and decisive. Basically, Satan said that Job would not honour God as he did if God weren't keeping him tightly hedged in with big blessings of wealth and health and family. That is when God gave Satan reign over all that Job possessed; but he could not take his life. In the blink of an eye, one messenger followed immediately by another, brought the news that all of Job's possessions, including his seven children, were gone. What does a body do with sudden catastrophe like this? "In all this, Job did not sin by charging God with wrongdoing." Job 1:22 (NIV) Then the chain of events repeated themselves, and Job lost his health, his body covered with painful sores from the top of his head to the soles of his feet. His response: "'Shall we accept good from God and not trouble?' In all of this, Job did not sin in what he said." Job 2:10 (NIV).

It was at this point that I felt taxed, thinking of all of this. So I decided to take a reprieve and check into my world, to take a wee peek at Facebook. There before me was a girl, standing against a fence, her back to me. She was mitted and hatted, protection against the cold of the north where she lives. Her long blond hair flowed down her back from out the confines of her hat. Her little sister stood tucked in tight beside her, which sister I could not tell. The beautiful northern scenery formed a breathtaking backdrop to the scene. Her mitted hand was reaching to pet the nose of their horse, Igby, who leaned down to her level to accept the offer of love. A heartwarming scene not at all like the picture of what I had just been thinking about; but as I let this play around in my mind, I knew that the same Sovereign God reigns in the northern regions of the country in which I live in 2014 as He did in the East those many years ago. I also know that Satan is still roaming to and fro challenging that reign. What was God doing in the space around these little girls as the picture was snapped? Was Satan right there trying to influence the scene, doing what he could to wreck the beauty? What do the big people in their lives do (me included) to build a hedge of deep awareness of God's love in them to protect them against that wily one? Whatever it is we should do, it must be authentic and real; it must come from the well of a deep acknowledgment of the Majesty of God.

This comes strictly from an amateur, but it would seem that Job spoke about 7500 words about his situation in the book of Job. It is hard to fathom what happened in Job's heart between the time in Job 2:10 when he said to his wife, "Shall we accept good from God and not trouble?" and the beginning of his 7500 words. The scripture says that Job opened his mouth and cursed the day of his birth. He said things like, "That day--may it turn to darkness, may God above not care about it...." Job 3:4; and in Job 3:25, Job says this: "What I feared has come upon me; what I dreaded has happened to me." What happened to Job between the time he spoke with such confidence of God's provision to his wife and the time when he uttered these words? When did the worry start?

In Job 6, Job longs for God to crush him, and then in verse 10, he says this: "Then I would still have this consolation--my joy in unrelenting pain--that I had not denied the words of the Holy One." Does Satan already know, and is Job onto something --that it is the day-in and day-out pain and problems that get us down, that cause us to turn against God? I don't know the answer to this phenomenon, but my faith is that God has something to teach us every step of the way and in the problems and in the pain is preparing us for the next step.

In Job 10:1, Job says the following: "I loathe my very life; therefore I will give free rein to my complaint and speak out in the bitterness of my soul." When I read this, my heart was cut; my gut reaction was, "Oh, Job, please don't say that. Look to the Majesty of God." However, within a minute or two I find myself focusing on some current aggravation. Are we all weak?

Four times in the book of Job, Job declared himself to be blameless. How did he come to that conclusion? God had declared him blameless. but why did he see himself in that light? To me, in the light of Romans 3:23 (NIV), "For all have sinned and fallen short......", this is a conundrum!

It took Job's three friends, Eliaphaz, Bildad and Zophar, about 3000 words to tell him all they thought they knew about his situation. They said some things that seemed to make good sense to me. For example, in Job 5:2, Eliaphaz says, "Resentment kills a fool, and envy slays the simple." Could it be that we would do ourselves a favour by paying attention to these words? Also, Zophar said this in Job 11:4: "You say to God, 'My beliefs are flawless and I am pure in your sight'." Is that the category into which I fall? Scary!! Again, in Job 20:3, Zophar says, "I hear a rebuke that dishonours *me,* and *my* understanding inspires *me* to reply." Is that where our long discussions about God lead us, our sureness of what He has done and how? Is the end of that journey self--*me and my? Scary again!*

In Job 32:1 it says, "So these three men stopped answering Job, because he was righteous in his own eyes." Elihu I will leave to the theologians.

In the beginning of Job 38, God takes the stage. It is interesting to me that it says He "spoke to Job out of the storm." Is that where we have to be before we will really listen to God? Begin to see His Majesty? In verse 2, God says to Job, "Who is this that obscures My plans with words without knowledge?" Could I be doing the same thing? Do I have the power to obscure the plans of the very Creator of the Universe in the life of another with my interpretations and analysis of what I think I know? Scary again! If my word count is even close to accurate, some 10,500 words were used up trying to convince someone else as to what God was doing! Isn't it interesting that, in the end, God asked tons of questions but gave no answers? They were not told the real reason for Job's suffering. They knew as much at the beginning of the story as they did at the end, and they knew all they needed to know: that God is sovereign. Does this story make me doubt God? Make me a little angry that God would allow such suffering? It did at one point in my journey, but not now. It is a miracle to me that God would trust us flawed, failing humans to help win this war against evil in the world, that He would trust us to be the conduit that brings the glory of God to the notice of another. May I focus on His Majesty and not on myself so that He can use me.

We love to sing the Christmas carol at Christmas, "Joy To The World." Have we-- have I internalized verse 4? It says, "He rules the world with truth and grace, And MAKES the nations prove the glories of His righteousness and wonders of His love." How many nations have risen, then fallen because they stumbled over the "glories of His righteousness", how many of any organization you can name, how many people? Did God treat Job fairly? Should He have allowed Satan to do what he did to Job? Would we include all of this story in our daily journal in the column entitled "Glories of His Righteousness"? Tough questions! To be answered in the deep recesses of our own hearts!

FB Post – March 29 2014

Job and I have been spending a good bit of time together of late. In his company is not the most delightful place to be--far too confusing. But it was likely that that spawned the thoughts that wandered through my mind as I sat in my chair in my snuggly housecoat, hot coffee cup calming the pain in my hands. The view from my window of our quiet subdivision is ever pleasant. Car lights made their way up the street as I looked; the still snow-covered rooftops of the houses down the street spread a white blanket before me. The tall trees stood, perhaps wondering just when in this year of 2014 they would be able to don their summer coats. And then the thought came, so very real, that in my next breath all this could be gone. I know that because it happened in the life of Job; it has happened in the lives of countless other people. What will my response be if that should happen to me? Will I still be able to say with calm assurance I love you, God?

CHAPTER 11

God in His mystery

MEDITATION: "The great mysterious work of the Holy Spirit is in the deep recesses of our being which we cannot reach." (Chambers, 1963)

Can you fathom the mysteries of God? Can you probe the limits of the Almighty? Job 11:7 (NIV)

I did not mean to remain with Job and friends into this chapter, but when I got to Chapter 38, I was so intrigued with the thoughts therein that I could not let it go. In Job 38:2, God says to Job, "Who is this that obscures my plans with words without knowledge?" Then in verse 3, God says the strangest thing! He says, "Brace yourself like a man; I will question you, and you shall answer me." When I think about this, I can't help but wonder how many times God may have said the same thing to me, but I wasn't listening. How many times have I argued about some biblical concept from my own understanding, when my understanding is always coloured by my humanness, by my background, by the people that I have paid attention to? Oh, to learn from God's confrontation with Job!

God's questions take up four chapters. There are seventy-one of them. I can see these questions published in a

Reader's Digest contest--the prize for one single yes answer being a return trip to the moon and back. There would not, I am sure, be a single passenger.

FB Post – August 25, 2013

"We will never know the joy of self-sacrifice until we surrender in every detail of our lives. Yet self-surrender is the most difficult thing for us to do." (Chambers, 1963). These are the first words I read this morning and they reminded me of something I saw on TV yesterday. The countries in the world whose students are scoring the highest in Math and Science are the countries that have made their programs harder for students to attain high marks. Is there a spiritual lesson in this for us as well? Are we constantly dumbing down the cost of discipleship in order to bring it into our comfort zone and, in so doing, losing the blessings that it has to offer? Would we be better off if, indeed, our focus was My Utmost For His Highest?

There was to be no dumbing down in God's questioning of Job. God's very first question in Job 38:4 is a zinger! God asked, "Where were you when I laid the earth's foundations? Tell me if you understand." Is this a little sarcasm from the lips of God? Then in verse 5, God asks, "Who marked off its dimensions? Surely you know!" But, God, surely You knew that Job didn't know, could not know. I don't know either. Do you? What does God want me to learn from this exchange? In Jeremiah 1:5, Jeremiah tells us this: "The Lord came to me saying, 'Before I formed you in the womb I knew you, before you were born I set you apart....'" Did God do the same with me? Did He somewhere along eternity's timeline make plans for me to be typing these words on April 14, 2014? Could this be the reason for the pit? What about what is happening in your life on this day? Has it been tucked in the Master's mind for eternity? I don't know. Do you? And what is eternity? How is it measured? Is it a straight line or is it circular? I don't know. Do you? I heard Leo Giglio, in one of his passionate lectures on the mystery of space say, "I am not trying to make you feel small. You are small." Is this the message God was trying to impress on Job's mind with His questions? I don't know. Do you?

There were more questions for Job--71 of them altogether, if I have counted correctly. Questions like "From whose womb comes the ice? Who gives birth to the frost from the heavens?" (Job 38:29) My humanity wants to add, "Did He get it right this 15th day of April, when the ground in our town was again covered with two inches or so of those frozen drops of dew?" Can you hear God's questions to us mortals in the year 2014? I can!

After 52 questions, God asked one more of Job. He asked, "Will the one who contends with the Almighty correct Him? Let Him who accused God answer Him." (Job 40:2) Job's answer: "I am unworthy--how can I reply to You?" (Job 40:4) For some reason, however, this confession was not enough for God, for He continued to question Job. Do you know why? I don't! I can only say it reminds me a little of John the Baptist sending the people, who had come to him to be baptized, home from the river with the command to bring forth fruit, meet [suitable] for repentance.

In verse 7, God said again to Job, "Brace yourself like a man, I will question you, and you shall answer ME." This is so strange, so full of mystery! God's first question to Job, again out of the storm, was, "Would you discredit my justice?" (Job 40:8) Scary!! Is that what I am doing when I complain about my lot in life, no matter what it may be? Right in behind that hard question, in the same verse, God asks another, equally as hard or more so: "Would you condemn Me to justify yourself?" Cut to the quick--that's what I am!!

After 18 more questions, most of them concerning the Behemoth and Leviathan, God closed with this in Job 41:34: "It looks down on all that are haughty, it is king over all that are proud." Why would God end this most important of times with Job with a description of a leviathan? I don't know. Do you?

What is this Leviathan, this Behemoth? I checked with Mr. Google and Mr. Wikipedia, and they don't know either--at least, not definitively. It would seem that what one decides that they were depends on what one believes they were. For me, I am happy to leave them in the realm of God's mystery. Whatever it is, it was at this point that some of the most beautiful words in all scripture are penned. In Job 42: 2 to the end of the chapter, I pen for you some of them. I am going to take the liberty to italicize those most precious to me.

"I know that you can do all things, *no purpose of yours can be thwarted....* Surely I spoke of things I did not understand, *things too wonderful for me to know.... My ears had heard of you BUT NOW MY EYES HAVE SEEN YOU. Therefore, I despise myself and repent in dust and ashes.*"

And so ends Job's story as I shed a tear; but this is not really Job's story, but a small part of God's story--God's story of love, of teaching us what we need to know in order to live fully in this sin-cursed, pain-inflicted world. Job's "stuff" was restored to more than he had before, his health was restored and a new family given. Is that, however, the real story? Did you notice that God never did reveal the REAL story, the real reason for his pain and suffering? What does that mean? I can only tell you what it means to me. God promised that we would not be called upon to endure more than we are able to bear. So for me, the question is, "Lord, what do you want me to learn from this?" Also, I need to realize that God may choose to use me in ways that I don't understand, and that the real reason may have little or nothing to do with me. God is Majesty, God is Mystery!

Read these four chapters of Job, with your heart and mind open and ready to soak up what is there; revel in the majesty of the great God who is speaking, catch the inflections and innuendoes of sarcasm and humour, see the pictures beyond the words, ride the emotional wave with the creative Creator, the mighty Maintainer, the royal Reigner, and you will forever be in love with this BIG,

BEAUTIFUL GOD who still knows how many hairs you have on your head.

P.S. My favorite? Job 38:36: "Who.....gives the rooster understanding?" LOL

Then there is the enigma of Solomon and of Peter and many others.

How could Solomon, the man with a gift of wisdom from God, be dumb enough to amass unto himself 700 wives and 300 concubines? Is Solomon's proverb, "Better to live in a desert than with a quarrelsome and nagging wife" (Proverbs 21:19), a reflection of this choice? I guess he should know. He likely had more than one in those 700 with that disposition. I really don't know. Do you?

As for Peter, I love him, this impulsive, passionate man. I wonder what it was like when he went home to his wife and said, "Honey, I met a man today who asked me to follow him. I'm not sure where I am going, but I have decided to go. So there may not be many fish from now on. Sure hope you and the kids do OK."

What must his fellow disciples have thought when they saw him go over the side of the boat to walk to Jesus on the water? Or when he denied that he knew Jesus and cursed and swore, what must they have thought? What did Jesus think? I don't know. Then, however, this impulsive, often foolish man, if historians have it right, chose to be crucified upside down rather than in the manner His Lord was crucified, and if Mr. Google has it right, that is the most painful method of crucifixion possible. How many times was Jesus exasperated with Peter? What did He see in Peter that caused Him to leave with him the keys of the kingdom?

Then there is the enigma of Jesus Himself. In John 1:1, it says, "In the beginning was the Word, and the Word was with God, and the Word was God." What? In the beginning? When was that? If the Word was God, must the Word not be eternal? When did the Word become un-eternal? Later the text tells us that the Word became flesh and dwelt among us. When he walked the earth, then, were the words He spoke God's words or His words? Or are they one and the same? I don't know. Do you? The "whys" and the "hows" belong to God, tucked away in His mystery. I love the mystery and what it means. To me, it means that I must get to know the Who! Someone--I don't know who--said that God's purpose in sending Jesus to this earth was that we might get to know what God is like and to emulate those characteristics as we find them. There are lots and lots that are evident as I take one more step closer to Him. Do I really want to be more like Him, do the work that I need to do for that to happen?

In his book <u>God Came Near</u>, Max Lucado (2004) has a chapter he calls "Twenty-Five Questions for Mary." I love these questions! Question 25 says this: "Did you ever think, *That's God eating my soup?*" I love this!! When I think of it in the light of Matthew 25: 35-40 [the judgment scene], then, yes indeed, should not we know what it is like to make soup for God? Surely we have all done something good for someone sometime. Does not Jesus say here that when we did, we did it to or for Him? Can you figure out how that works? Just what channels does that good deed go through to get to the Creator of the Universe? I can't figure out how this works, but I trust it does! The realization of that touches every good deed and gives it a new perspective, a divine perspective, and in the doing, we become better people. A very happy mystery!!

My mother's favorite hymn was "God Moves In A Mysterious Way" (Words by William Cowper, Music by Thomas Ravenscroft). These words deserve our careful reflection. The following is verse 5:

Blind unbelief is sure to err

And scan his work in vain.

God is His own interpreter

And He will make all plain.

Psalm 31:14,15a: "But I trust in you, Lord; I say, 'You are my God'. My times are in your hands."

I want to live in His Mystery, recognize there is probably very little that I really know and be content to live in that empty space, trusting Him. It takes a load off!

From Wilderness to Wonder

We cannot kindle when we will

The fire which in the heart resides.

The spirit bloweth and is still,

In mystery our soul abides;

But tasks in hours of insight willed

Can be through hours of gloom fulfilled.

(Chambers, 1963)

CHAPTER 12

God in His mercy

MEDITATION: "Show me, Lord, my life's end and the number of my days: let me know how fleeting my life is." Psalm 39:4 (NIV)

He lifted me out of the slimy pit, out of the mud and mire, he set my feet on a rock and gave me a firm place to stand." Psalm 40:2 (NIV)

As I sit poised to begin this chapter, it is Easter weekend, 2014, and my mind drifts to Hagar, to the woman taken in adultery, to all the Prodigal Sons who have gone on before. I can't help but wonder what they would tell me of His mercy if they could.

One such person was one of the readers I "met" (as mentioned in chapter 6) through my grandson who, in 2012, was involved with others in putting together a CD of 100 Bible passages (some just a verse, some more) read by 100 different people from the church he attended. One of the readers was an old man with a quavery voice who read the 23rd Psalm. I know not the man, cannot picture what his wrinkled face might have looked like. I never met him, but I dearly love him. The inflections and cadences of his voice just seemed to sing out, "And I know the reality of all these words." He passed away not long after, his reading of those words became a reality for me and others to listen to. I can't help but wonder, if I could hand him a pen or a keyboard and ask him to insert into this chapter his feelings about the mercy of God, what would he write? One day I will ask him.

Hagar's story in Genesis is a "'tear your heart out" kind of story. Her life unfolded in ways that it would be hard to see her deserving. She was an Egyptian girl, either bought or just taken, to be servant to Sarah, the wife of Abraham. When Sarah got up in years and still had no children, she took matters into her own hands. She gave Hagar to Abraham for his wife and then sent her to bed with him. In other words, Hagar was treated as an object to satisfy the whims of another human being--never a good idea because it never works out. God's way cannot be thwarted. Hagar did indeed became pregnant, with the result being jealousy and bitterness in both her and Sarah's heart. Sarah became so mean to her that Hagar could no longer stand it and ran away. How long this slave was in the desert, how old she was when this happened to her, I don't know, but I suspect she felt afraid, alone and unloved with probably a very low concept of her real worth. Why do we humans do these sorts of things to each other? Do we even recognize them for what they are when we do? It is not God's way. God sent an angel to minister to her. It would seem to me God's message to her wouldn't be too comforting. The angel told her she would have a son, a son named Ishmael (meaning "the Lord who hears") because the Lord had heard of her misery. This son would be like a wild donkey and live in hostility with all his brothers. In Genesis 16:13, it says: "She gave this name to the One who spoke to her: 'You are the God who sees me.'" She went on to say, "I have now seen the One who sees me." The name for God that came from this is El Roi. How could Hagar accept all of this and not fight back? Is it that she saw God's mercy in her circumstances and that was what mattered to her? Whether the circumstance was hard or easy was not part of the equation. I don't know. I do know that I wish that I had known her.

Max Lucado in his book <u>God Came Near</u> (2004) talks of a mercy he calls "severe mercy." In talking about it, he talks of one of Satan's most powerful tools—"the agent of familiarity." He tells of his little daughter almost drowning in a pool, how that near-death experience woke him up to the appreciation he really felt for so many of the familiar people and things around him, and he now makes sure to do things that will never let him forget. God's mercy does not always show itself in flowers and flowing ribbons. Often a jolt of mercy is needed to show us who we really are and what we are really chasing after. Somehow I feel that was the reason for my pit. I am glad I had that time.

FB Post - September 8, 2013

As I sit in my chair, lumpy with age, in my familiar room my world is pretty small. But even in the small town in which I live, apparently the second safest place in all of Canada in which to live a battle is going on concerning the use of some public buildings--each side, I am sure, believing they are right and the other wrong. Across the greater world, high level meetings are being held to decide which weapons will be used and when to use them, to lift up right and get rid of wrong. We "stand our ground" and fight for our concept of "right" at every level--in our homes, in our churches and schools, in every facet of our lives. Into the fray comes a loud and thunderous voice, and if we would listen, we would hear Him say this: "Can you make a mountain? Can you tame the wildest animals of the jungle and have them lie at your feet?" And in an instant that thunderous voice becomes a baby born in a dirty stable, a homeless, wandering man never demanding His rights. Then He is gone, leaving the Spirit of the thunderous voice, the Spirit of the homeless man to help us sort it all out, to help us be the peace we need in our homes, in our churches, in our schools, in our world, yea in our own hearts in order to make alive His message of peace, of selflessness, of service for another's good, of mercy.

In John 8, we find the story of the woman taken in adultery. Who was this woman, anyway? We are told little. What we are told is that previous to this story, the guards, the Jews, the Pharisees and even Nicodemus were involved in controversy as to whether to arrest Jesus or not. Then Nicodemus spoke up and suggested to them that even their own law would not condemn a man without first hearing from him as to what he had been doing. Their response in John 7:52 (NIV) was this: "Are you from Galilee, too? Look into it, and you will find that a prophet does not come out of Galilee." Your God is too small, Mr. Pharisee! Perhaps you are right; I do not know one; but even if you are right, that does not prevent God's mighty hand from raising one up from the place of His choosing at the time of His choosing. Or so I think!! Aren't we so like these Pharisees? I read somewhere not long ago the suggestion that the Pharisees' greatest problem was not their hypocrisy, but that they had no concept that they could be wrong. That thought was way outside the sphere of the possible for them. Could it be that that is the most productive snare that Satan has for us? We are still much like Eve --we want to be sure we know as much as God knows! Was that not the problem that Job and his friends had? Isn't it funny that the last person in the world we humans want to get to know really well is ourselves?

After these Pharisees and leaders had exhausted every effort to find justification to arrest Jesus, the text tells us they went home. Jesus then went to the Mount of Olives. I will leave it to you to judge what He might have been doing there. The text tells us that at dawn He returned to the temple courts. The crowds gathered around Him again and He sat down to teach them. That is when the teachers of the Law and the Pharisees dragged in a woman, thrust her before Him and informed Him that she should be stoned for she had been caught in the very act of adultery. The text informs us a little later that they did all of this in order to trap Jesus. In other words, they were not interested in her good nor her family's, not even the justification of their own laws and religion. Only to get rid of someone who was telling them something they didn't want to hear. OUCH!! In other words, she was being treated much like Hagar had been treated so long ago. OUCH AGAIN!!

What did Jesus do? He put the onus of fixing the problem right into the hands of those who wanted it fixed. He gave them the instruction and gives us the example that the place to start the fixing is in the depths of our own hearts. You know the story! He called on the accuser free of sin to cast the first stone. They all left. He then told the woman He did not accuse her. What?! An adulteress unaccused? He then told her to go and sin no more. It is interesting to me that He did not do anything, or so the text appears, to change whatever the circumstances were that she was in, which may have been worse than it had ever been when she returned home. Merciful He is, loving enough to give us what is needed to make us long for Him. God always sees in His children what His children so often miss in each other. He sees the potential!!

FB Post – Feb. 10, 2014

I pressed the right button on my Kindle to open <u>My Utmost For His Highest</u> to February 10 and this hit my eyes: IS YOUR ABILITY TO SEE GOD BLINDED? The scripture Mr. Chambers sent me to was Isaiah 40 where I read the following: "Lift up your eyes and look to the heavens. Who created all these? He who brings out the starry host one by one and calls each of them by name. Because of His great power and mighty strength, not one of them is missing". (Verse 26) And I can't even keep track of my glasses. That should put what I think I know in perspective. And do I hear God giggling?

AND THEN THERE WAS THE PRODIGAL SON! You know the story. There are so many lessons of God's mercy in this story. Here are some that I see.

1) God does not forcefully supersede our own will. He will let us go down, down, down all the way to the pigpen if that is what is needed to turn us back in the right direction. Even God cannot save us from ourselves.

2) He really, really wants us back home with Him. Waiting for the prodigal, He stood with hands over His eyes, chasing out the light so that He could see as far as possible, waiting through the pleasant days and nights, but also the stormy days and nights of rain, hail and sleet--waiting to welcome his boy home if he ever came.

What a picture!! What took the boy so long? Could it be that we all instinctively know God's perfect goodness and our own perfect un-goodness? Is our "going home to God" prideless, selfless, sorrowful--a Job's dust-and-ashes experience or is it simply an affirmation of something we have been taught? There was no doubt in the prodigal's mind. There should be no doubt in ours. From thence comes the peace that passes understanding.

Husband had a childhood/teenage/college friend who, though he was crippled from a childhood disease, had great musical talent and plenty of charisma. Because of this he was everybody's darlin'. He could persuade a radio manager to let him come in and perform on the radio at the drop of a hat. Give him a dollar and he could turn it into a million almost overnight. He went to college, married, had two children, made big money, divorced and the downward spiral had begun. He had lost his wife and the big money was to disappear in gambling soon after. Soon everything was gone. Except for cancer! Cancer came! Like the prodigal he headed back home--back to God. In that journey he wrote and made a personal CD of a piece he called "The Day I Saw God Run." I share a part of it with you here:

Like the Prodigal of old, I threw it all away;

I wasted my soul, life was just a game to play.

Then when I came to myself and
I knew what I had done,

My Father ran to meet me. That's the day I saw God run.

(Chorus)

I saw God run the day that I was on my way back home.

I had promised Him so many times, I'd never, ever roam.

Weary, so unworthy but He smiled and called me son.

I'll never, no I'll never forget the day I saw God run.

Have you seen Him run?

CHAPTER 13

I am the bride

MEDITATION: The earth is the Lord's, and everything in it, the world, and all who live in it, for He founded it on the seas and established it on the waters. Who may ascend the mountain of the Lord? Who may stand in His holy place? The one who has clean hands and a pure heart, who does not trust in an idol or swear by a false god. Psalm 24: 1-4 (NIV)

I have helped to ready several brides for their bridegroom in that I have made several wedding dresses, including my own. The last one I made was for a niece and by far the most challenging. The dress was made of raw silk, with $125.00 per yard embossed lace layered over the bodice and sleeves. The lace had two sizes of flowers on it, one a little larger than the other. It was deemed by me, the bride and the bride's mother that the centre of each of these flowers should be accented with a small pearl. The neckline, the empire waistline and the bottom of the sleeve edges were all accented with a continuous row of these embossed flowers. The bride's mother and I spent the better part of a day on our hands and knees on my living room floor, laying and re-laying these flowers on the train, trailing them down each side of the train and gradually filling them in to form the perfect medallion effect around the bottom of the train. All the things needed to make this dress were purchased in a bridal shop which sold readymade wedding dresses as well. The clerk had assured us that pearls did not need to be sewn on, just glued. Before we had left the store, however, she made the mistake of letting it be known that she swept up oodles of pearls every day that had fallen from wedding dresses as they were tried on. The decision was soon made in my head and heart that the pearls on this dress would be sewn on. When I made that decision, I did not know that, including the headdress and veil, the number that I would sew on added up to more than seven hundred. Preparing a bride for a bridegroom takes a lot of effort in many different areas. How much more effort should it take to prepare the bride for the bridegroom when the bridegroom is God the Word, Jesus Christ?

In John 3 (NIV) we find Jesus baptizing, and as the followers of John the Baptist said, everyone was following him. John's reply was that the bride belongs to the bridegroom, that he had been sent as a servant to the bridegroom, and when people heard the voice of the bridegroom there would be much joy. He went on to say he had heard that voice and felt the joy. A reading of these verses leaves little doubt that he is referring to Jesus, to God the Word in the flesh.

I love Acts 2:47 (NIV): "And the Lord added to their number (KJV--church) those who were being saved." If I love God, if I believe, if I have obeyed, then it is God Himself who makes me a member of His great family. What other identification do I need? If I am His, if He has made me His bride, how intimate should my relationship be with Him? Someone somewhere said we should be *sleuthing* for God. *Sleuthing*--not a very charming word. When you try to say it, saliva rolls from your tongue and drops in great uncomfortable pools in the bottom of your mouth. Perhaps that is indicative of what our journey will be like to get to the place where we can feel at home with the great God of the universe. Is that why the churches that dot the landscape across this country, where 67.3% (Statistics Canada, 2013) of its people claim to be Christian, are emptying faster than water flows from a bucket with a hole in the bottom? Is the journey just too hard for most of us? Are there just too few of us who have ever seen God run? Or is our emphasis on the wrong things? I don't know, but I think it must surely make God sad. If I am the bride, then my love, my devotion, my all must be for the bridegroom.

I often wonder what that very first fledgling church after Pentecost must have been like. Most, if not all, of those people would have either helped crucify Jesus, would have seen Him crucified, or would have known somebody who fit into either one or the other of those categories. Can you imagine the tone of their gathering? I think there would have been tons and tons of hugs, oodles of tears of deep emotional gratitude, hands raised in jubilation for the resurrection. I doubt there would have been too many complaints about the weather floating around, or complaints of how bad the government was and so on and so on. It didn't take Satan long, however, to find them and, as the historian said, Jesus feet had barely left the earth when the power struggle began. The fight has been going on now for over 2000 years, and as a result, a recent comment I saw on the internet read something like this: "Christianity? I have never bothered with it. All those people ever do is fight with each other." If I have been added to God's family by God Himself, if I am His bride, it behooves me to do all I can to make that bride as beautiful as possible. How can I do that?

August 23, 2013

I am so thankful this morning for a lady named Antionette who found herself, in the middle of her ordinary day doing her job as an ordinary bookkeeper, faced by a gunman with an arsenal enough to destroy all in the school she was working in. She faced the gunman, not with more violence, but with the deep Spirit of God within her, with mercy and compassion for the gunman, with a deep love and care for the children in the school that transcended her own safety. And because she did, not a single person was hurt. I pray that her story will be told over and over again until it makes a difference in the adversarial halls of our governments, on the adversarial streets of our cities, in the adversarial nooks and crannies of our towns and countryside, to the adversarial nature of our churches, and yes, to the adversarial nature of my own heart. There was a man who walked the earth long ago and showed us the way.

Please, may I have your permission to use my pearl-covered wedding dress as an allegory to illustrate something else that I see in it? Let the raw silk represent us as we come into the world, first and foremost made in the image of God. Just like much of that silk is pure beautiful silk, there are some lumps in it, there is some discolouration in it. So with us! We have weak areas because of the sin nature of this old world we are coming into. It behooves each of us to become aware of those weaknesses and let God fix them. But so often we do not! We are too proud to admit that any of the 3D's, or P's or Q's, whichever one plagues you, could be weakness in US. Many times these weaknesses come from the sin nature of generations before us, but sooner or later we reach the stage in our life when we have to take them as our own and let God reverse the trend. Usually, though, we don't. We try to cover it all up and make ourselves look good with that $125 per yard lace. Also, the flowers on our lace come in all different shapes and sizes. Sometimes in the shape of money in the bank, sometimes a pretty blue dress, sometimes pride in our long hair or short, whichever we prefer, sometimes in pride of our children or grandchildren, a big, fancy car or house. On and On!

Are we willing to let the Master Seamstress/Tailor take His divine sewing needle and stab with the sharp point through the centre of our flowers to that pure silk underneath to add the needed pearls to make us beautiful? Will we grant Him that right, all the while knowing that the sharp point of His needle will hurt, sometimes make us cry or scream? Job could tell you how it feels!

Hebrews 4:12 tells us that "The Word of God is alive and active. Sharper than any double-edged sword, it penetrates even to dividing soul and spirit...." Our temptation as humans is to get into a discussion, trying to nail down what the difference is between soul and spirit. I don't know what it is, but whatever it is, I'll bet it hurts. I'll bet if my nightie could talk, she would let us know that she wasn't too happy being flopped from side to side, banging with each flop against the hard surface of the washing machine, but she needs it in order for her to be clean. We need the sharp tools that God has at His disposal in order for us to be clean.

So what would be the pearls that God would add to the flowers of our lace to make us truly beautiful? Of course, I cannot know for sure; I am not God. I suspect, however, that they would come in the pearl of "do unto others as you would have them do unto you"; in the pearl of "it is more blessed to give than to receive"; in the pearl of "love your enemies"; in the pearl of "turn the other cheek"; in the pearl of "be pure in heart"; in the pearl of "consider others better than yourself." Then would come the big pearls of "the fruit of the spirit". They would fill the centres of several flowers. Then there would be two very large and beautiful pearls sewn in such a place and in such a way as to bring the maximum amount of beauty to the bride's garment. One would be the pearl of "love God with all your heart and soul and mind" and the other would be "love your neighbor as yourself."

Then comes the question: If I am the bride of Christ and He has adorned my garment with all this beauty, even though I still need oodles of His grace for it to be seen, then what do I do? Do I don it on Sunday morning and go share it with 3000 or 130 or 30 similar brides and we congregate and congratulate each other on how nice we look, on what good people we are, on how we're glad we're not in the same state as some wandering around without their garment? I am afraid if that is all there is, I will be like the brides who tried on the dresses with the glued on pearls. They will simply fall back off and I am left wearing a garment that is phony.

Romans 12:1 in <u>The Message</u> says: "So here's what I want you to do, God helping you. Take your everyday, ordinary life--your sleeping, eating, going-to-work, and walking-around life--and place it before God as an offering. Embracing what God does for you is the best thing you can do for Him." The NIV version of the Bible calls this activity "your true and proper worship." When do I "go to worship"? If I am His bride, "worship" is, as Louis Giglio would say, "the air I breathe."

I visit a dear, ninety-one year old lady in the Nursing Home. She often says to me: "Oh, Wilma, I just love my Lord." Recently she was feeling bad because: "But here I sit. I am not going to church."

I said, "Marjorie, I think when you and I sit here and we encourage each other in our love for God, that that is a church service." (where two or three are gathered together in my name)

She said, "Oh, Wilma, do you really think that?" and I said that indeed I do. She then said, "Oh, Wilma, that is beautiful." And it is beautiful! It is beautiful if shared with one sweet lady, whose space on earth is but enough room for a single bed, for her big chair, for a walker that turned the right way makes a chair for me to sit on while I visit and one small closet to hold her clothes. The real beauty of this "beauty" is that it easily transposes itself to a group of twenty gathered in a home, to five thousand on the side of a hill, or to thirty thousand in the most modern building imaginable in the richest suburb of the richest city in the country. It is the heart that matters, the heart in tune with God reaching out to another heart in tune with God, and His Spirit works mightily in the fellowship, and we are encouraged to climb a little higher, to love a little deeper, to present our bodies in worship a little more consistently. Then I said to my sweet friend, "But we do have a problem. Who is going to get the collection?" We laughed together and I felt that I heard God laugh just a little.

I am the bride, be I here or there.

FB Post - Oct. 30, 2013

One doesn't need either good eyes or good ears to be aware of some of the controversies that swirl around regarding "church". But when I think about it, my mind's eye sees again and again the sweet lady who comes to my house every Monday morning. It is sometimes hard to watch her make her way up my street because she walks with a big limp. She comes in and struggles to remove her coat with only one hand to help. The other hangs limp at her side wishing for the ability to lend a hand. But the ability is not there. You see, she had a stroke in her early 20's. She moved to my neighbourhood less than a decade ago, she and her husband choosing this as their retirement community. Only a year or two slipped by until he had passed away leaving her alone with only a little dog to help take up the slack of a lost good leg, a lost useful hand. She comes in, we settle in our chairs. I tell her of some profound thought I have found in my early morning readings, her song is always the same: "God has been so good to me." How could she say that in her circumstance? I don't know! I only know that I am encouraged, find strength in her strength to move forward. And "church" comes together, "worship" happens. No doctrine to defend, no funds to raise, no programs to plan. Just we, two people who love God, with Him in the midst (where two or three are gathered), spiritual growth takes place. We will do it again next week. I already know all the words of the sermon. And it will be good.

CHAPTER 14

The rim of the hill

MEDITATION: You will keep in perfect peace those whose minds are steadfast, because they trust in you. - Isaiah 26:3.

As I gaze at my garden from my kitchen window, I am enthralled. The ligularia in the back corner, his huge leaves taking up more than his share of space seems to shout, "You didn't know I would grow this big, did you?" The columbine dips her pink head just enough to be coy and cute. The "bordered with white bias tape" hosta leaf wants to be sure that I know he is a leaf in his own right, not just part of a mass of green. The just-home-from-the-greenhouse coral bell settles into her spot waving her pretty peachy, pink leaves in the breeze. It draws me to the point that I have to leave my duty at the kitchen sink and move into the yard for a closer look. When I do, however, I see a different picture--not the dream picture from the kitchen window, but the reality of the garden. The hosta leaves have been a sweet snack for the slugs, the pink columbine's dark blue brother's growth is stunted because he is in the wrong place, and his colour is not right for such a shaded garden. And then there are the weeds!

So I return to my duty at the kitchen sink, but my eyes are drawn again to the garden, and soon I am looking just beyond the garden into the darkness of the shade of the trees and the never ending (it seems) depth of a hill. My eyes follow the darkness of the hill to the top--to the rim of the hill. Only when I let my eyes go as far as the rim of the hill and higher do I finally see the light. As I stood and contemplated all of this, it began to dawn on me how what I was seeing in my garden was so much an analogy of my own spiritual journey. Perhaps it is also of yours.

I thought of that perfect garden from afar as representing all those things that have looked so good to me from afar--a new person that I had met and I thought how happy I would be if that person was my friend, some clothing item that I just knew would make me lovely, a trip that would be the most pleasurable thing that I might ever have done. After a while they are mine, but they never seem to satisfy.

The darkness of the shady hill represents the place that looking for complete fulfillment in anything of this earth takes me. The person, or thing, or work may be good, but no matter how good, our search for fulfillment in anything outside of God Himself will take us into darkness.

My eyes followed the darkness to the "rim of the hill." Funny! The rim of this particular hill is a place of death, the cemetery where lie the physical remains of my Mom and Dad and countless other Moms and Dads, aunts and uncles, brothers and sisters and people's children--all just over the rim of the hill. I say "Funny!" because most of us would think of "a place of death" as being a descent, not an ascent; but the experiences of my life, the things that I am learning on my spiritual journey are teaching me otherwise. Luke 9:24 says, "For whoever desires to save his life will lose it, but whoever loses his life for My sake will save it." Just before life there is death; just before the light there is the "rim of the hill."

Whether we are dealing with despair or disease or waiting to cross through that final death (which we all are), maybe we need to lift our eyes to the "rim of the hill", but this time let's make the ascent up Golgotha's hill. Let's fix our eyes on the scene of death. Can you see with your mind's eye that cross, now standing empty? Then lift your eyes to the mighty light beyond. That will put all the "gardens" of our life into perspective and we will find contentment with Him. (Written August 15, 2009)

"When I think about my salvation experience, I think of being delivered from sin and gaining personal holiness. But salvation is so much more! It means that the Spirit of God has brought me into intimate contact with the true person of God Himself. And as I am caught up into total surrender to God, I become thrilled with something infinitely greater than myself." (Chambers, 1963)

I have contemplated these thoughts from my original story, along with Mr. Chambers' constant reminder that we must give up the right to ourselves; contemplated them much since 2009. The garden is still there, still draws me to it when the flowers are at their best. Like me, it has changed over the years. The ligularia still takes up lots of space and its family has grown tenfold in five years. The little pink columbine left us long ago to find a living place more to her liking and she took her brother with her. The "not so sure of who I am" hosta has been chastised more than once and made smaller, only to come roaring back and in need the chastisement yet again. A pretty, fuchsia pink phlox was invited in by someone (I know not who) and has made her home tight to the stone wall halfway up the hill. The darkness still saddens as I look into it, and soon I raise my eyes yet again to the rim of the hill. Death is still there--often sad, sad death. But so is the light beyond still there. So is the empty cross, but I see something different in that cross now. I see it as my cross!

"Whoever does not take up his cross and follow me is not worthy of me. Whoever finds their life will lose it, and whoever loses their life for My sake will find it." Matthew 10:38-39.

This, indeed, sounds like a climb up that dark hill to the rim, to the place of death. Death to self--no more right to myself. His song must become my song, my very own! The tentacles of ugliness must be brought out into the open and given to God so that I can breathe. I must see God's will for my life as far more important than my own comfort; I must not fall into the trap of those dumb mice. I must see my circumstance, be they hard or easy, as God's tool preparing me for something I cannot see, and I must accept them in humility. I must pick up that cross that I still see standing on the top of the hill and carry it with gratitude, with a passion for God, with self-control and with trust. And in the doing, I must have hope--hope of God's triumph after a while over the 3D's of this life.

FB Post - June 8, 2013

I read a phrase just now that caught my imagination--"God wants you to be something that you have never been." Wow!! On this 8th day of June, 2013, after living 76 years, 260 days God wants me to be something I have never been. What kind of a journey am I on? A pretty awesome one, I think. And there are no body scans, no baggage checks, no lineups to get aboard. All that is required is a heart available to God. What will I be by the end of the day, June 8, 2013, that I have never been. I'll let you know.

Psalm 40:8 (KJV) says, "I delight to do Thy will, O my God...." I love this word "delight." It fosters images of pleasant sights in my mind, like the first colour of fall in the trees; it fosters the remembrance of sounds that touch the heart like water flowing over the rocks as it makes its way to the sea; it fosters the excitement of surprise when I discover three fuchsia phlox plants in my garden and I don't know where they came from; it fosters pure heart-bursting love when we experience one of those "first smile for Daddy" times. All these and more are the components of "delight." Then why on earth did the Psalmist use this word to describe his feeling in doing God's will? God's will is the stuff of self-sacrifice, of killing the natural self-centeredness in ourselves, of turning the other cheek, of giving when it is hard to give, of pushing ourselves to do just one more thing for that person who may never appreciate it. I think it is because when we do these things, God in numberless ways at the strangest of times through the most surprising people drops a huge big chunk of "delight" in our path and we are forced to stop and say, "Where did this come from?" When we take the time to meditate on that question, we know the answer and the "delight" of obedience grows within us. (Written January 31, 2012)

FB Post - May 31, 2013

I just finished sewing together two thousand, five hundred and fifty-eight small triangles. I did this using what Quilters call the Paper Piecing Method. That means I stitched carefully along a drawn pattern line on paper with the fabric on the back. I did this with sight in only about half of one eye. As I was nearing the end of this project I had my TV on as I sewed, I heard a young 16-year-old play the piano and sing beautifully. This young man was playing with only three fingers on each hand, with problems in his elbows that greatly curtailed the use of his arms. The interviewer asked him if he had any advice for others with difficulties. His answer: "Figure out a way to do what you want to do and then don't quit until you accomplish it." Many times my project was so difficult that I wanted to quit. But I am glad I didn't. It was important that I finish it--it was a labour spawned by love. You see, this quilt is for my granddaughter.

Our delight in obedience, in carrying our cross, must also be spawned by love--love for God, love for others. If it hasn't been spawned by love, it will soon be nothing more than legalism, an empty shell that hurts rather than helps.

I love Hebrews 12:1-3. Here Paul admonishes us to throw off *everything that hinders*. We know from other places that this admonition includes Father, Mother, Children and yes, even to the plucking out of our own eye. It is an all-encompassing admonition. Then in our "getting rid of", he calls for us to get rid of the *sin that so easily entangles*. In his book, 66 Love Letters, Dr. Larry Crabb says this: "We must learn to hate sin more than we hate suffering." (Crabb 2010). Jesus did, didn't He? The text tells us that He endured the cross, like many others in those days endured crosses.; but it was the shame (the sin) that He hated, that He scorned, that caused Him to cry out as One alone. And, indeed, He was alone!! Not even God could be with Him carrying all that load of sin. Though I was not a living person then to join Him at that cross, I am now!! But, oh! I so seldom do! Perhaps that is the reason that so much of our life is lackluster. We do not really see His cross, so we fail to pick up ours. He picked up His with joy-- FOR ME! I WILL do my best to pick up mine. For some strange reason, I have the promise that it will be light and easy. Not without sweat, blood and tears, but light because we have a vision of the joy that will be ours if we do..

I have a dear friend who lives in South Africa. She comes to Canada about once a year to visit family here. When she comes, she almost always comes to my house for my husband's southern breakfast, and she brings the family with her--seven, in all. We love these visits! A year or so ago, she brought me a lovely, pink violet. As they were leaving, I thanked her for the violet a second time. Her response was, "Give it a drink of tea. They love tea." So I did--and still do! All left-over tea is saved. I have even been known to make a pot special just for the violets. The result, you ask? They grow and grow and bloom and bloom. They never stop blooming! I know you aren't supposed to transplant violets when they are blooming, but I had to. They were grown right out of the pot and still always blooming. When I did, I was sure I had killed some of them. They were dumpy for a day or two with dumpy flowers on them, and then they perked up and took off growing and blooming as if nothing had ever happened. All because of a cup of tea!

When I was thinking about this I thought, "What would it take for me to give some soul the 'tea' they need for them to take off growing spiritually and blooming for the world to see just how God's love works in us? And what would I need from that someone for the same thing to happen in me?" This is what it will take for our walk with the Lord to turn from an exercise of duty that doesn't satisfy--just a wilderness of doing the right thing instead of becoming a beautiful, growing plant full of colour so that we can give colour to the world. How can we help each other to grow?

My friend, Don Smith posted this on FB: "If people feel you are a welcoming, safe and empathetic person then conversation will be taking place. Often very deep conversation....experiences of pain, loneliness, exclusion and disconnect. Any question is safe...because you are safe. Having an inclusive, yes, spirit is a welcome sign for many. You are a blessing."

And so I leave you, dear reader. I leave you with the deep-seated confidence, with the deep-seated hope that I can trust Him in His majesty, in His mystery, in His mercy. May you feel the same.

EPILOGUE

FB Post - Oct. 18, 2013

Her name is Maya Faith. Her face will remain a mystery until Papa's birthday--so he hopes. Maya Faith. I roll her name over my tongue and I am glad I know it. Oh, I know, the ladies down the line are saying to themselves and perhaps to others, they shouldn't have made it public so soon. But I am glad they did. I think of it and wonder when God first called her Maya Faith. And when did He share it with the angels and did they immediately compose a song to sing back to God of Maya Faith. Knowing her name gives me the strength to square off once again with that basher of beauty and focus on the majesty and mystery of God. Names! I think of special names down through the years who have helped me see God – of Paul Tournier and Philip Yancey and Fred Smart, of Aunt Amy and Aunt Emma, of Don Smith and Dorothy Dennis, of Ann Voskamp and now of Maya Faith. And my heart sings.

REFERENCES

Allender D. & Longman T (1999), The Cry Of The Soul: how our emotions reveal our deepest questions about God. Colorado Springs, CO. Navapress Publishing Group

Chambers, Oswald (1963), My Utmost For His Highest. Grand Rapids, MI. RBC Ministries/Discovery House Publishers

Cowman, Mrs. Charles (2004) – Streams In The Desert, Zondervan.

Crabb, Dr. Larry (2010), 66 Love Letters, (Sorenson, Kierkegaard,Provocations. New York. Plough Books, 2007). Nashville, TN. Thomas Nelson Inc.

Dobson, James (2012). When God Doesn't Make Sense. Tyndale House Publishers

Kapat-Zinn, Jon (2010) Wherever You Go, There You Are, Mindfulness Meditation In Everyday Life, Hyperion e-books.

Lincoln, A. Quote from www.goodreads.com.

Littauer, F. (2001). Personality for Couples. Unerstanding yourself and the one you love. Grand Rapids, MI. Baker/ Revell

Lucado, Max (2004). God Came Near. Nashville, TN. Thomas Nelson Inc.

Mandela Nelson, (1994) Long Walk To Freedom. London, England. Little, Brown & Co

Nouwen H. (2001).Finding My Way Home: Pathways to Life and Spirit. Pathways Publishing NY.

Peterson, E. (2006). The Message.Colorado Springs, CO, Navpress Publishing Group

Piper, John (2003). Don't Waste Your Life. Wheaton, ILL. Good News Publishes/Crossway Books.

Phillips, M (2012). Dawn of Liberty. Bondfire Books, LLC., Colorado.

Shakespeare, W (2003). Hamlet. Simon & Schuster

Tournier, Paul. www:goodreads.com

Weil, S. (2003), Gravity and Grace. Taylor and Francis

Lightning Source UK Ltd.
Milton Keynes UK
UKOW01f1808100616

276071UK00001B/54/P